What Movies Can Teach Us About DISABILITIES

Trevor Pacelli

Published by Pacelli Publishing
Bellevue, Washington

What Movies Can Teach Us About Disabilities

All rights reserved. No part of this book may be reproduced or transmitted in any form or by any means, electronic or mechanical including photocopying, recording or by any information storage or retrieval system, without the written permission of the publisher, except where permitted by law.

Limit of Liability: While the author and the publisher have used their best efforts in preparing this book, they make no representation or warranties with respect to the accuracy or completeness of the content of this book. The advice and strategies contained herein may not be suitable for your situation. Consult with a professional when appropriate.

Cover and interior designed by Pacelli Publishing

ISBN 10: 1-933750-58-8
ISBN 13: 978-1-933750-58-3

Copyright © 2022 by Trevor Pacelli
Published by Pacelli Publishing
9905 Lake Washington Blvd. NE, #D-103
Bellevue, Washington 98004
PacelliPublishing.com

Table of Contents

Preface 4

Introduction 7

Chapter 1: Blindness...11

Chapter 2: Little People...27

Chapter 3: Facial Disfigurement...43

Chapter 4: Autism...59

Chapter 5: Limb Loss/Difference.......................................75

Chapter 6: Mental Illnesses...91

Chapter 7: Memory Loss...107

Chapter 8: Motor Impairment..123

Chapter 9: Mutism...139

Chapter 10: Deafness...155

Conclusion..171

Appendix 175

Acknowledgments...184

Notes..185

Index 215

Preface

"A person who has a physical or mental impairment that substantially limits one or more major life activities, a person who has a history or record of such an impairment, or a person who is perceived by others as having such an impairment."

- The definition of a disability according to the Americans With Disabilities Act of 1990

The first known cinematic depiction of disability was an 1898 Thomas Edison short called, *The Fake Beggar,* and since then, as the art of moving pictures evolved into the behemoth industry we know today, public awareness of disabilities evolved along with it.

The Job Accommodation Network compiled a list of around seventy-eight disabilities, not including subcategories of disabilities, so as you could imagine, a massive majority of them are either underrepresented or hardly represented at all in film. For the purposes of this book, I won't dedicate entire chapters on the disabilities that only have a tiny handful of films that represent them, just the ten that I found are most common.

The disability community makes up the world's largest minority group—over 57 million disabled Americans make up the over 1.3 billion disabled people who live on Earth. The 2019 US Census data furthermore estimated that twenty percent of Americans have a disability, and ten percent have a visually obvious disability. Although some may take offense to the word "disability," since it draws attention to what they lack rather than what they can achieve, deafblind advocate Haben Girma has said that she doesn't believe the word should be considered offensive since it's synonymous with "civil rights."

She also believes that the disability itself is no barrier, but rather that the real barriers happen across social, physical, and digital settings, such as the lack of ramps at a beach. She furthermore says that prejudices toward a disability often come from fear, such as feeling that death is more appealing than living in a wheelchair or having a prosthetic limb. She furthermore says that humans are naturally designed to be adaptable, even in a culture that isn't doing enough to accommodate those unique needs.

As somebody on the autism spectrum, I know how modern American culture can casually shun people with disabilities. Back in high school, I was cast in a play as part of my drama club, yet I was the only actor in the entire cast with no lines at all and only walked across the stage for about thirty seconds total. The director told me my part had the possibility of being expanded, but it never happened.

The play had an opening dance number that I was meant to participate in, but the choreographer instead shoved me aside (on purpose) and gave me no part in the dance besides sitting on the side and watching. Overall, what could have been a fun, wonderful experience became my worst memory of high school; during this time, I particularly wanted to commit suicide.

I'm telling you this because I believe it's a perfect example of what it looks like to be included but not accepted. A child with a disability can be "included" per se in a group with all the "normal" kids, but that won't save them from being shoved off into a separate corner away from the others. I've seen that happen at all of my schools, where the special needs kids, such as those with Down Syndrome or severe forms of autism sat at isolated lunch tables and were ignored at recess or other group social times. Organizations act in similar ways, generating a public illusion of allowing everyone the same privileges, even though behind the scenes people are still not included equitably.

That is why I'm motivated to write this book, so together we can make sure that fewer kids or adults have to go through what I went through.

Introduction

"The disability community is the only minority group that anyone can join at any point in life for any reason, and if a person lives long enough, they are likely to experience disability of some kind."

- Lamar Hardwick

Having grown up a Christian, I learned about the stories of Jesus healing the blind, lame, deaf, and mute. Looking back, I believe the messages were lost on me, as the stories seemed to be used by the church to inspire nondisabled listeners. I grew up with the idea that disability is a disease and must be looked down upon by everyone, which altered my thinking up until now.

That stigma stuck with me on the family vacations of my youth. When my family went to Walt Disney World after I turned nine, we met some of their friends, and my mom told me beforehand that a man there had lost some of his fingers. I was so afraid to lift my face and see the man's hand that I kept my face down inside my book the whole time.

Then in third grade, our family went to one of those Ripley's Believe It Or Not! museums while on vacation. It was so scary for me that I couldn't make it to the end, my mom had to take me back outside. But my parents kept a pamphlet from the museum, which I looked through a lot after coming home. Without the frightening atmosphere of the museum, the photos in the pamphlet simultaneously scared and intrigued me.

Once in a while, I'll look through one of those Believe It Or Not! books to be frightened and intrigued all over again, looking at all the people with rare birth defects and sideshow acts with cruel stage names such as "Mule-Faced Woman," "Lobster Boy," and "Monkey Man." I was even more exposed to what most people would call "the world of circus freaks" by television specials on Travel Channel I watched as a teenager, with one-of-a-kind cases titled, "The Turtle Boy," "The Tree Man," and "The Octopus Man." As a bonus, there were those *Guinness World Record* books that contained certain records such as "longest nose," "shortest man," and "oldest conjoined twins," which I remember catching the attention of me and my classmates back in second grade.

However, nothing ever taught me to show sympathy toward people with those kinds of differences until I was in seventh grade, when my mom, sister, and I watched *Extreme Makeover: Home Edition*. Nearly every episode featured a family where one or more members had some disability or illness, of which my twelve/thirteen-year-old self was mostly afraid of. Although I was hardly ever scared by movies, seeing bodily disproportionate people like the ones on TV would be among my biggest fears.

I hope that reading this book will help open your mind and your heart to just how far we still have to go to consider ourselves a disability-accepting world. Likewise, my view of disability still needs work, as I still often catch myself staring at passersby on the street who may be in wheelchairs, wear a prosthetic, or have Down Syndrome.

Even with the movies I love, many of them are listed here as negative examples of disability representation. With a heavy heart, I needed to accept that there are some politically incorrect things about *Star Wars, Harry Potter, Amadeus, RoboCop, Braveheart, Men in Black,* and *Pirates of the Caribbean: The Curse of the Black Pearl*. However, I feel my duty as a film critic is about separating my own bias in favor of the facts. To recognize why the problem happens, we need to look within ourselves to see the source of that problem.

Oh, and there will be spoilers for almost every motion picture mentioned here!

Discussion Questions

1. Do you have a disability?
2. If yes, what's a big misconception people have about your disability?
3. If not, do you have a friend or family member with a disability?
4. Do you prefer disability-first language (an autistic man) or person-first language (a man with autism)? Why?
5. Do you think it's ethical for a nondisabled actor to play a disabled character?
   - What's an instance where a movie character with a disability could only be played by a nondisabled actor?
   - What's an instance where a movie character with a disability was played by a nondisabled actor, but the part would have been better if it was played by an actor with the same disability?
6. What are your top 10-20 favorite movies?
   - Of those movies, which ones feature a character with a disability?
   - Does the actor playing that character with a disability have a disability him/herself?
7. Was there ever a movie that got you angry over the way it portrayed a disability?
   - Why did you think it was so damaging to disability representation?
8. Was there ever a movie that you loved because of how it portrayed a disability?
   - Why did you think it was so beneficial to disability representation?

Chapter 1: Blindness

My Personal Experience

In thinking back to my childhood, I don't recall knowing of any blind people at school or anywhere else; my only exposures to the blind community are limited to three media properties:

The first is a blind girl named Marina from the hit TV series *Arthur*, who made a couple of appearances as the friend of a character named Prunella. One of those episodes taught kids the dos and don'ts of treating friends with disabilities, such as not trying to be too helpful unless they specifically ask for help.

The second is from *Pokémon: Ruby Version;* in this game, there were three ultra-rare Pokémon, Regirock, Regice, and Registeel, who needed to be obtained by decoding a series of puzzles with braille descriptions. Being the Pokémon geek I was back in sixth grade, I was so desperate to get to these three legendary beasts that I made my mom drive me to the library to check out a book on translating braille... only to find out the dictionary we had at home already had a braille translator! Whoops!

The last is Toph, the blind earthbender from *Avatar: The Last Airbender*. She used earthbending (or moving rock and dust with her mind) to create a mental picture of her surroundings by using the ground's vibrations felt through her bare feet. Back then, I didn't care much about her, mostly because I was a dweeby tween who believed her blindness made her incomplete. Later as an adult, I rewatched the whole series on Netflix, and Toph essentially became my favorite character, not just because of her rough n' tough personality, but also because of how she turned her disability into an advantage to become "the most powerful earthbender in the world."

Ultimately, I was a pretty privileged kid back then who wasn't able to consider the struggles of the blind community, which was much different from what I've learned in my research for this book. For instance, I discovered that when seeking out accommodations, blind people often lack authority when requesting accommodations from schools and workforces. Among those blind people raised by sighted parents, it's common for their parents to think little of what their supposedly handicapped child can accomplish, in turn depriving them of fruitful experiences.

Fortunately, groundbreaking resources to help blind people enjoy life have become available over the last several decades, including text-to-speech phone apps, machines translating written/spoken word into braille, 3D Sound Maps, and audio description receivers. There's even a version of baseball for blind people: "Beep Baseball." Even then, these breakthroughs aren't always enough, because sighted people must help to ensure easier communication with those who need the technology.

For instance, if someone who is blind needs to read an email using text-to-speech technology, and the email is full of typos, the speech command vocalizes that accordingly, and it ultimately leaves the blind listener confused. While going through revisions for this chapter, the low-vision reader I had proofread my earlier draft mentioned how I need to make sure I use lists to help the text-to-speech technology pick up the words as separate points, not as one continuous line of text.

So before going deeper into what I learned about the spectrum of blindness in film, here are some essential facts to know about the disability:

Quick Facts

Types of blindness, which eyeglasses cannot improve:

- Total darkness, or No Light Perception (NLP): 15% of people with eye disorders fall into this.
- Light Perception: Light can be seen.
- Congenital Blindness: Blind from birth.
- Legally Blind: When one has a visual acuity of below 20/200 on the Snellen Chart or a visual field of below twenty degrees (also referred to as "Tunnel Vision").
- People who lost eyesight sometime after birth.

Other surprising statistics (at least to me):

- In 2015, around 253 million people worldwide were low-vision, only 36 million of which were blind.
- In 2018, it was estimated that 13% of adult Americans were low-vision even with glasses or contact lenses.
- In 2016, it was estimated that 22.3% of blind or low-vision people had never finished high school.
- Around 70% of blind or low-vision people are not employed full-time.
- 65% of blind Americans are married, while 16.5% of them have divorced.
- 10% of blind people worldwide can read braille, and only 0.9% of blind Americans can read it.
- 2-8% of blind people use a white cane, the rest use either guide dogs or nothing whatsoever.
- It's possible that 20-30% of blind people use echolocation.
- 90% of blindness is curable or preventable, but many have no access to the treatment.

The Film in Focus

Title	City Lights
Director	Charles Chaplin
Writer	Charles Chaplin, Harry Carr, Harry Crocker
Main Cast	Charles Chaplin, Virginia Cherrill
Studio	Charles Chaplin Productions
Country	United States
Release	7 March 1931
Runtime	1 hr. 27 min.

Synopsis

A down-on-his-luck Tramp (Chaplin) meets a beautiful blind girl (Cherrill) who spends much of her time on the street selling flowers. Then he saves a millionaire from committing suicide and produces a system to leech from his wealth by intoxicating him with alcohol. The Tramp in turn uses this to his advantage as he tries to swoon the blind girl, fooling her into thinking he's rich... until he discovers that she and her grandmother are in deep financial trouble, and he has to find odd jobs to help them.

Alas, he's unsuccessful in getting the blind girl the money she needs. After a misunderstanding between himself, the millionaire, and the police, the Tramp ends up in jail, but only after he's able to transport a considerable sum of money to the girl. Months later, he's released from prison, and he sees the girl in her new and improved state: a steady permanent job in a flower shop, and most important of all, she spent the money on a cure for blindness that the Tramp found in a newspaper ad. They now can live happily ever after together!

The Film's Portrayal of the Disability

While going through other young actresses to cast for the blind girl, Charlie Chaplin met twenty-year-old Virginia Cherrill at a boxing match. He felt she was the perfect fit for the part because she had mannerisms similar to a near-sighted person. Yet when filming began, he and Cherrill did not get along too well; the scene where their two characters first met broke a Guinness World Record for the most retakes for a scene... 342 times! But the immense toil paid off, as *City Lights* continues to be a success well into the twenty-first century.

When the American Film Institute updated its list of the 100 greatest movies of all time in 2007, *City Lights* made it to #11, compared to #76 in the original 1998 list. The movie also made #38 on the AFI's list of the 100 funniest movies, #33 on its list of the 100 most inspirational movies ever, #10 on its list of the 100 most romantic movies ever, #1 on its list of the 10 best romantic comedies ever, and the Tramp made #38 on its list of the 50 greatest movie heroes.

However, does anyone from the blind community agree with the mostly sighted movie lovers who claim that this is an all-around perfect movie? Now, I'm not blind, so I can't speak for them on that, but I can certainly talk about how the dated cinematic qualities of *City Lights* lead to poor storytelling, which naturally ignites an aura of social irresponsibility.

Plenty of the narrative cues around *City Lights* are designed to suggest that this blind girl is helpless by herself. She lives with her grandmother and needs help with everything—her independence is out of the question. But when she meets the Tramp, she assumes that he is a rich man, and this Tramp just takes advantage of her blindness to play off this misunderstanding.

While skimming through the paper one day as he visits her home, the Tramp sees a headline: "Vienna doctor has cure for blindness!" After a series of chaotic events, he gives her some stolen money for that cure, then months later, she gets the cure, which opens up the door for her successful job running a floral shop, instead of just sitting on the street trying to sell flowers. With all these prerequisites met for a socially acceptable woman, the unnamed blind girl becomes sexually desirable to the Tramp. Never is her blindness seen as something to accept, but rather as a disease that must be cured. That's not the worst of it: the Tramp is ultimately rewarded for exploiting her disability.

Not only is her blindness seen as undesirable, but something to mock too: In one scene, she pulls some yarn that gets caught through the Tramp's shirt, but she cannot see the source of the yarn, so she thinks she's raveling it casually. This gag serves no narrative purpose other than to make fun of her blindness.

Aside from being dehumanizing, Charlie Chaplin's depiction of blindness is also inconsistent. The blind girl seems to make eye contact with the Tramp upon their first meeting, but afterward, she never makes eye contact until the end when she can see. (This error still happens with blind characters played by sighted actors in movies and TV shows today, such as in the TV series *In the Dark*.) Also, sometimes she carries a cane while out on the street, and sometimes not. These inconsistencies prove that nobody working on this film did much research on what blindness is actually like.

It doesn't seem to be any secret that Charlie Chaplin made this passion project of his for other sighted audience members, not for any blind audiences. He only made it as an attack on the rise of cinematic sound, which he feared was killing the art of cinema. It's nice that he respected the filmmaking arts, but what if an actual blind person wanted to spend a night at the theater in 1931? It could have been a tremendous sigh of relief for them if they found out movies could finally make noise, providing a way for them to experience the cinema by using their sense of hearing.

But if a film back in 1931 was silent, there would be no other way to accommodate blind audience members other than someone else next to them verbally describing everything on screen (which would be met with shushes from annoyed moviegoers in the theater). This was decades before audio description receivers were invented, and back in the day, TVs and computers weren't invented yet either, so once a movie left theaters it was gone forever. Thus, in this rare case of blindness being represented on screen, the actual blind community couldn't experience it.

The Disability in Film History

Other films about blindness may have been made before *City Lights,* but it's certainly the oldest well-known one. Unfortunately, the negative impact of Chaplin's blind girl character is still apparent today in terms of blindness on screen. In these examples of ways that blindness can be depicted in movies, note which ones of these are also found in *City Lights.* As for the ones not found in *City Lights,* think about what cultural influences may have led to these harmful stereotypes.

The Obstacle Trope

The most common portrayal of blindness is as an obstacle that a victim (usually the hero) would need to overcome. This includes Jamie Foxx's Oscar-winning portrayal of Ray Charles in *Ray*, but this also includes Han Solo's carbonation sickness at the start of *Return of the Jedi;* despite his condition of temporary blindness, he still manages to rescue his friend Lando from the Sarlacc pit, making him look more heroic. Likewise, in *The Matrix Revolutions,* Neo's eyes are electrocuted in a fight against Agent Smith, leaving him blinded. Yet this condition doesn't weaken Neo like Smith thinks it will; this blindness is only there to open up the big reveal of his ability to see another's energy, cementing him further as the Jesus Christ figure for the Matrix.

The Masseuse Trope

Other movies have tried narrowing down the jobs available for blind people into only one stereotypical occupation, such as a masseuse, as seen in *The Masseurs and a Woman, The Tale of Zatoichi, At First Sight, Happy Times (2000),* and *Zatōichi (2003)*. Little known fact: Japanese masseurs were at one point traditionally blind so a client wouldn't have to feel embarrassed by a stranger rubbing their naked body. Yet the impression behind this stereotype is that the blind community should only stick to specific jobs, leaving more space in other fields for nondisabled workers.

The Victim Trope

Robin Hood (1973) has the titular hero on two separate occasions disguising himself as a blind beggar to leech a little more coin offerings from the rich to give to the poor. While his intentions are good, this mockery of a blind person, complete with sunglasses, a cane, and old rags for clothes, makes people with that condition look poor and helpless. Then there's the scene in *Slumdog Millionaire* when Jamal recalls a blind beggar boy asking for money, which only benefits Jamal as he answers a question on *Who Wants to Be a Millionaire* about whose face is on the hundred-dollar bill.

Then *Scent of a Woman* features a colonel who lost his eyesight while in war, yet the treatment of his character is more that of a cranky old man who's had enough of life. His blind condition, complete with the familiar cane and sunglasses, gives an image that anyone with his condition is in a living hell and would rather just put a bullet to his head. More of this poor mistreatment happens in *Johnny Got His Gun,* which will be covered in later chapters.

The Superhuman Trope

While this does mean well in making someone use their disability to their advantage, it's ultimately just using it to make awesome action fighters, be it Daredevil in *Daredevil (2003),* Xiao Mei in *House of Flying Daggers,* or Chirrut Îmwe in *Rogue One: A Star Wars Story.* This isn't like Toph in *Avatar: The Last Airbender because* that show also presented her other struggles as one with a disability. In the case of these three examples, there's no apparent struggle in their lack of seeing, it's just so they could be cooler fighters while their other senses get a power boost.

And while this film is popular amongst the Christian community, *The Book of Eli* also proves troubling in the way it ignores the blind man's struggles as he goes about his journey in this post-apocalyptic world. His blindness seems more like a ploy to make him even more inspirational like an "underdog" story with an unlikely hero—the only one left who knows the words of the Bible. He could have been a seeing character and nothing in the plot would have been affected much.

The Comic Relief Trope

Although still a hilarious classic that's perfect to watch on Christmas day, *A Christmas Story* proves to be rather problematic in how it dresses Ralphie up in his daydream like a stereotypical blind man, with sunglasses, a cane, and a tin mug for begging. More offenders include the three blind mice in the *Shrek* series and Billy Ray Valentine imitating a blind beggar in *Trading Places (1983)*. Then there's Blind Al from the *Deadpool* movies… a crabby old woman whose blindness is the only component of her personality, and half of the lines directed at her or said by her are jokes about her absence of vision. More of this can be found in *Mary and Max* with Max's neighbor, who's mostly just there for comic sight gags rather than to be a character.

The Villain Trope

Villains having some disfigurement has been a trope in Hollywood for ages and partial blindness is probably the second most common villain trope. Think of all the villains out there who have a scar over one eye: Ernst Stavro Blofeld in the *James Bond* series, Tony Montana in *Scarface (1983)*, Scar in *The Lion King (1994)*, Hopper in *A Bug's Life,* Le Chiffre in *Casino Royale,* and the Knave of Hearts in *Alice in Wonderland (2010)*. Regarding movie villains who are flat-out blind, there's Blind Pew in *Treasure Island (1950),* both the Bullet Farmer and the Coma-Doof Warrior in *Mad Max: Fury Road,* and Norman Nordstrom in *Don't Breathe*.

Blind People Feeling Someone Else's Face

A particular romantic subplot in *Fantastic Four (2005)* features a blind woman who feels Ben Grimm's (aka: "The Thing's") rocky face, which is an important turning point for him because it's finally a sign of someone accepting him despite his hideous appearance. There lie two problems with this scenario: 1. The blindness is only there to make the sighted character feel better about himself. 2. Almost no blind person feels a stranger's face in real life, they couldn't care less how others look. That case of a blind person feeling one's face is also found in *The Miracle Worker (1962)*, as that's what Helen Keller is seen doing with Miss Anne Sullivan's face, especially when first meeting her.

The "Other" Trope

The Bride of Frankenstein features a blind old man who lives alone in a little hut, and he's the only one who warmly welcomes and accepts Frankenstein's monster. Since the man cannot see and the monster cannot speak, they form a connection, further associating blind people as being different, and thus, at the level of monsters. It's like Mr. Mertle in *The Sandlot,* who is just a scary, mysterious neighbor who's keeping all these baseball secrets in his house. On that same note, at the start of *The Curious Case of Benjamin Button,* a story is told about a blind engineer who built a clock. The idea of making the man blind just to put him in a position of constant isolation, giving him more time to work on something as ambitious as a giant clock, is the opposite of disability inclusion!

*****

But well-made movies about blindness do exist:

Life on a String (1992) - *China*

As depicted during a time when blind people were shunned from society, two blind men, a saint alongside his young companion, Shidou, seek out the secret formula to restore their vision. Over those many years, Shidou falls in love, while the saint starts to wonder if retrieving his sight is worth the trouble. Even if they may never see the stars or the blue sea, both men discover the inner peace of accepting their worlds, each of which has a different aura of beauty than the world outside themselves.

Blindsight (2006) - *United Kingdom*

Six blind Tibetan teenagers take the impossible challenge of climbing Mount Lhakpa Ri, a voyage led by Sabriye Tenberken (founder of Lhasa's first school for the blind) and legendary blind mountain climber Erik Weihenmayer. The difficult trek leaves painful tears to be shed, but the team eventually proves their potential and reaches their goal together! After the great trek, one of the teens expands his living as a masseuse to open Tibet's biggest massage clinic, as well as a cold drink business.

Notes on Blindness (2016) - *United Kingdom*

Coming from John M. Hull's original audio diary, his tape recordings are used in place of traditional dialogue, which the actors dub their lips to. This ambitious creative choice powerfully conveys his desire to pinpoint the purpose of blindness. Since going blind, his memories start to fade away, and he falls down a path nobody else can follow—not even his wife. Yet this cinematic autobiography ultimately delivers a powerful testament to the true tragedy of blindness.

Get Out (2017) - *United States*

Jordan Peele's groundbreaking horror flick proves the potential danger of someone without vision wanting something more than what he already owns, to the extent he would essentially kill to get it. That character is Jim Hudson, the blind art dealer who wins the gamble of having his brain dissected into Chris's body. From a narrative perspective, it works to make him, being the blind character, a minor character so that the audience sees the victim's perspective of how a disability could become toxic.

AndhaDhun (2018) - *India*

Akash sets an experiment for himself: If he feigned blindness for life, would that help inspire his piano music? Then one day, he witnesses a murder that he must find creative ways to expose without giving away his true condition. Yet the woman involved in the murder finds out about his big lie, which she fights back at by permanently blinding him for real. It's made clear how much Akash screwed up, by faking a disability for his selfish means, in time the karma struck him badly.

*****

If you want to find ways to learn about what blindness is like, these five movies are ideal. While it's not only limited to these five, nor should these be your bible in understanding blindness, these are still suitable places for you to start as you learn beyond the stereotypes about a minority group you may not be a part of. Now, to help you think more critically about all you just read, here are some questions:

Discussion Questions

1. The film in focus, *City Lights,* has been named one of the greatest American films in history. Do you agree with this statement? Why or why not?
2. Looking at the types of blindness at the start of this chapter, which one do you think the blind girl in *City Lights* has? What evidence makes you reach that conclusion? How does that specific categorization of blindness affect the treatment of her character?
3. How would you change the ending of *City Lights* so that the Tramp is properly punished for taking advantage of the blind girl? How would this alternate ending change the film's portrayal of blindness? Would it be better, worse, or unchanged?
4. Imagine an alternate ending for *City Lights* where the girl doesn't get her blindness cured. How would this alternate ending change the film's portrayal of blindness? Would it be better, worse, or unchanged?
5. Watch a movie mentioned in the section, "The Disability in Film History." Do you agree or disagree that the movie is a negative depiction of blindness? Why?
6. *Life on a String:* Go to a place with a beautiful landscape view and close your eyes. Pay attention to what you hear, feel, and smell. Would you say then that blindness is a total loss? What would that say about blind people who would want to find some cure for their condition?
7. *Blindsight:* These teenagers were bullied and shunned by everyone, and were even considered cursed by the religious leaders, told that they were blind as punishment for something they did in a past life. Think about your

past interacting with others who have a disability. Did you treat them like this in any way?

8. *Notes on Blindness:* John Hull had all sorts of concerns about being blind, one of which was that his parents would neither recognize nor accept him. Does this surprise you about how a blind person would think? Upon watching this movie, what else surprised you about the mental state of a blind individual?
9. *Get Out:* How many blind people do you think wish they could cure themselves? How many do you think are content with being blind? What makes you think that?
10. *AndhaDhum:* Go outside and close your eyes. Can you make music out of what you hear? What do you think this tells you about how blindness can be an advantage in creativity?
11. Upon watching all these good examples, are there any you believe shouldn't be considered a good example?
12. Now, onto some personal takeaways. Put on a blindfold and turn on a movie you've never seen before. Keep the blindfold on throughout the whole movie. Just rely on your sense of hearing to pick up the story. What is this like for you? How does this change the way you think of other blind people?
13. What new/surprising knowledge did you pick up from reading this chapter?
14. What's the biggest misconception you just learned about the blind community?
15. And most importantly: How will you start to live differently having a new perspective on the blind community.

Chapter 2: Little People

My Personal Experience

I remember loving *The Wizard of Oz* as a kid. The munchkins scared me back when I was four because at the time I didn't understand that some people have a condition that makes them smaller than usual. While it wasn't enough to scare me out of watching the movie, the small people with disproportionate body parts and plastic hair singing like they were on helium left an unpleasant impression on my toddler self. I was always happy whenever it got to the part when Dorothy left Munchkinland because it meant the scary part was over.

Throughout the rest of my childhood, television and film were the sole influences that exposed me to anyone shorter than five feet. I saw so many little people playing roles where their height demanded it that I became numb to it. Such roles from movies I used to love included the goblins from *Harry Potter,* some of the whos from *How the Grinch Stole Christmas,* the Oompa Loompas from *Charlie and the Chocolate Factory,* and many funny TV commercials where a little person played an elf, troll, or any other little fantasy creature. Then of course there was the famous, "He's an angry elf" scene from *Elf* that still has me on the floor laughing even after the hundredth viewing.

The few times I did meet someone in person with dwarfism, my treatment of them fell much more on the dark side. I remember in my sophomore year of high school when I constantly made fun of a cheerleader who (I guess) had dwarfism, with a shoe size of only two. I wasn't the only one: one student asked her, "Do you need a ladder to pick up a penny?" She also was teased for being able to fit inside a locker. Looking back, I'm so sorry I stooped low enough to join in on the bullying of her and other peers who were shorter than average. My exposure to various media was a massive influence on my belief that little people should be the butt of every joke, and are only half-human (no pun intended) compared to a person of average height.

In my adult life, however, things were a bit better. While my exposure to little people was rarer than in high school, I still had some moments. For instance, one time I browsed through GameStop, a customer service representative asked if he could help me out. This man clearly had dwarfism, although I kept mindful to just speak to him normally, even while I was thinking, "I thought he was a kid at first!"

Plus, a good friend at my church has told stories about how he was going to be a dwarf. Before he hit puberty age, he had to take medication designed to rapidly increase his growth so he would end up of average human height rather than a dwarf. He described the experience as being full of indescribable bodily pains, like regular growing pains times a hundred. It's interesting now for me to think of that; I had never heard of medication used to prevent dwarfism.

Nowadays, I occasionally glance out the window while I'm driving and see someone shorter than five feet tall, and don't acknowledge them, which is currently the only exposure to little people I ever get. So I needed to put in lots of research for this book, as before I started work on this chapter, I didn't even know that the word "midget" is considered an offensive term to describe little people. Other little people treat that word like calling a Black person the n-word, yet it's still casually used in today's culture by many able-bodied people...

Quick Facts

There are around four hundred varieties of dwarfism, which is usually defined as being 4'11" or shorter. The most common types are:

- Disproportionate: When some parts of the body are typically proportioned but others aren't. For instance, the person may have a regular-sized torso but shorter-than-average arms and legs.
- Proportionate: When all parts of the body are equally smaller than average.

Among the causes of dwarfism:

- Achondroplasia: This makes up 70% of all cases and alters the growth of the cartilage and bones.
- Diastrophic: This causes bone disfigurements, particularly resulting in a cleft palate, shortened forearms, and/or smaller calves.
- Spondyloepiphyseal Dysplasias (SED), A bone growth disorder that can also cause vision and hearing problems.
- Turner Syndrome: A type that only affects females.

Other important facts:

- Little People of America (LPA) has stated they prefer to be referred to as dwarfs, little people, people of short stature, or having dwarfism.
- The main condition most people with dwarfism need help with is osteoarthritis, otherwise, it's reported that nearly all people with dwarfism can do almost anything a person of average height can do.

The Film in Focus

Title	Freaks
Director	Tod Browning
Writer	Willis Goldbeck, Leon Gordon
Main Cast	Harry Earles, Olga Baclanova
Studio	MGM
Country	United States
Release	20 February 1932
Runtime	1 hr. 4 min.

Synopsis

A beautiful trapeze artist, Cleopatra, develops a romance with a little person who also works at the circus, Hans, although he is already engaged to another one of the circus' little people, Frieda. Cleopatra only wants to marry Hans to inherit his immense fortune, so she conspires with the strongman, Hercules, to kill Hans after their marriage.

The wedding happens, and at the following dinner party with all the other performers of the circus, Cleopatra slips some poison into his drink. Yet Hans sees a drunk Cleopatra kiss Hercules, so he realizes she does not love him and passes out. While bedridden, he decides to manipulate Cleopatra while the other sideshow acts plan their revenge by turning her into one of them: a legless, tarred, feathered "Human Duck."

Months later, Hans is in his mansion with his fortune, yet guilt-driven because he feels responsible for Cleopatra's fate. Frieda comes to visit him and ensures him it was not his fault, and that she still loves him.

The Film's Portrayal of the Disability

Other names *Freaks* was rereleased under included *The Monster Story, Forbidden Love,* and *Nature's Mistakes.* Labeled as a horror picture for its use of "real freaks," Tod Browning (a former sideshow actor, and director of 1931's *Dracula)* directed MGM's piece of shock cinema to capitalize on the horror boom, using the most shocking subjects of terror: people who don't look like the common folk. These included but weren't limited to:

- Jane Barnell (who had a full beard)
- John Eckhardt Jr. (who did not have the lower half of his torso)
- Elizabeth Green (who had no apparent disability aside from looking a little odd)
- Daisy and Violet Hilton (who were conjoined at the hip)
- Josephine Joseph (who was supposedly half man-half woman)
- Martha Morris and Francis O'Connor (neither of which had arms)
- Prince Randian (who had no limbs)
- Angelo Rossitto (a little person who later founded Little People of America)
- Simon "Schlitzie" Metz, Elvira Snow, and Jenny Lee Snow (who all had microcephaly)
- Isaac W. Sprague (who had muscular atrophy)
- Minnie Woolsey (who had Virchow-Seckel syndrome)

Plus, the main cast starred two dwarf siblings, Harry and Daisy Earles. These two, alongside their two other siblings (who made up a theatrical group called "The Doll Family"), played munchkins in *The Wizard of Oz!* Harry was the blue Lollipop Guild dancer.

The finished product was intended to be ninety minutes long until a disastrous test screening forced around a half-hour of shocking footage out of the final edit, now lost forever. The movie's premiere wasn't much better; it's been reported that on opening night, the audience turned ill while others ran out in fear. Many of the actors who played the sideshow acts later voiced disdain toward the motion picture, particularly Jane Barnell, who became an activist for the disability community.

So long story short, *Freaks* was an absolute failure of an experimental film that destroyed Tod Browning's career, it was even banned from the United Kingdom, only to finally be released in the 1960s with an X rating. It was during that time when *Freaks* gained eventual classic status thanks to the counterculture circuit and hippie movement.

Many would argue this movie was ahead of its time, and maybe it was, as this possibly marks history as one of the first times someone with a physical disability appears as human, even displaying his character flaws. At the start of the movie, Hans refuses to take a woman's orders, then by the end, he learns differently. The other sideshow acts likewise live in ways that defy stereotypes: the conjoined twins take romantic likings to separate men, the bearded lady gives birth to a child, and the performers without arms can do things just as well as a person with arms can do, such as lighting a cigarette. And of course, one of the little people is very rich.

However, there's still greater evidence of mistreatment from the film crew toward the actors who played the "freaks." The script features instances when the able-bodied actors make ingenuine compliments toward the differently-abled actors, but they are patronizing in their context. It's part of the negative messaging behind *Freaks* that makes people with disabilities look like monsters.

The treatment of little people gets the worst of it. Besides how much more frequently Hans is mocked for his height than praised for his character, Frieda is also seen hanging up laundry for a woman of average height, giving the imagery of her as a slave. Plus, the film's tagline is: "Can a Full-Grown Woman Truly Love a Midget?" That sounds like a rhetorical question suggesting that little people should stay with their own kind.

What's even more devastating is that a majority of movies throughout history, even those coming out today, aren't a whole lot better. Those assumedly dated concepts of disability in the "freak show" setting are still at work today. Just recently, I found an old-fashioned shooting gallery in Seattle, and on its walls were vintage posters saying: "See: Bodies Joined Together, Siamese Twins, 4 Arms, 2 Legs" and "The Frog Boy: 36 in. Tall Alive, Never Walks: Hops Like a Frog." This was 2022, and there was still a clear acceptance of "circus freaks" being put on display, and movies being made today still like to treat the little people community that very way.

The Disability in Film History

The depiction of little people in cinema is perhaps the most commonly depicted disability. Little people have been exploited across every film genre imaginable, especially in the sci-fi/fantasy genres to fit inside a creature costume or a little compartment to create special effect tricks. Consequently, those narrative purposes had harmful dehumanizing effects on the viewers.

The Supernatural/Fantasy Creature Trope

The munchkins in *The Wizard of Oz*, the Oompa Loompas in *Willy Wonka and the Chocolate Factory*, the medium in *Poltergeist*, the dwarfs in *Willow*, some of the whos in *How the Grinch Stole Christmas*, the goblins in the *Harry Potter* series, the dwarfs in the *Chronicles of Narnia* series, the elves in *Fred Claus*, and the dwarfs in the *Hobbit* trilogy have used little people to play small magical beings. Little people have also played fully costumed little creatures, such as the Jawas and Ewoks in *Star Wars*, the troll in *Troll (1986)*, Hoggle in *Labyrinth*, the rodents of unusual size in *The Princess Bride*, the goblins in *Troll 2*, Cousin Itt in *The Addams Family (1991)*, Howard the Duck in the box office flop of the same name, and two dwarfs who helped bring E.T. to life.

The Comic Relief Trope

Amadeus features a bunch of little people in a vaudeville musical number. *Spaceballs* has little people play "Dinks" (or Mel Brooks' version of Jawas). *Braveheart* has two short men put on a humorous reenactment of an execution. *Friday* features a little person chasing a regular-sized man. Mini-Me from the *Austin Powers* series is designed strictly to ignite laughter as a miniature version of the villain. Jason "Wee Man" Acuña from the *Jackass* franchise has his height emphasized numerous times. *Bad Santa* has a foul-mouthed dwarf dressed as an elf who gives rude, snappy remarks that draw further attention to the fact that he's a dwarf. *The Wolf of Wall Street* turns dwarfs into darts because Jordan Belfort and his friends think they're "built to be thrown." And finally, Marvel throws a Peter Dinklage cameo into *Avengers: Infinity War*, making him a giant so audiences could laugh at the familiar short celebrity finally being the tallest in the room.

The Villain Trope

Danny DeVito, who has Fairbank's disease, often gets the worst of this treatment, as he's been cast as the Penguin in *Batman Returns*, the father in *Matilda*, a corrupt journalist in *L.A. Confidential*, and a neighbor from hell in *Deck the Halls*, of which in that role his wife is played by Kristin Chenoweth, an actress also well known for being short. Other examples include the title role in *Leprechaun*, Ginarrbrik in *The Chronicles of Narnia: The Lion, the Witch, and the Wardrobe*, Corpus Colossus in *Mad Max: Fury Road*, and Nick Nack in *The Man with the Golden Gun*, which Mini-Me from *Austin Powers* is based on.

Short Cartoon Characters

Examples of this include Mr. Huph in *The Incredibles*, Aloysius O'Hare in *The Lorax*, and Professor Poopypants in *Captain Underpants: The First Epic Movie*, all of which are villains. Yet there are villain sidekicks included in this too, such as the King of Hearts in *Alice in Wonderland*, Smee in *Peter Pan*, and Lefou in *Beauty and the Beast*. These short emasculate characters are there only to generate comic sight gags next to the much bigger, much scarier main villain. Seldom are short cartoon characters seen as good guys, and even then, they're neither the main character nor meant to be taken seriously; examples include Yao in *Mulan*, Jane's father in *Tarzan*, Edna in *The Incredibles*, and "Shorty," the little man dressed like Cupid in *Tangled*.

The "Freak" Trope

There have been plenty of movies about either the circus or clowns that depict little people playing sideshow stars, including *The Greatest Show on Earth, Johnny Got His Gun, The Elephant Man, The Greatest Showman, Joker, Nightmare Alley (2021)*, and

Elvis (2022). Plus, there have been two cases of Danny DeVito getting cast as a ringmaster in a Tim Burton movie: *Big Fish* and *Dumbo (2019)*. These cases embrace the concept that little people are the quickest way to represent the weird setting of a circus.

The Victim Trope

By the third act of *Joker*, Arthur (a.k.a. "Joker") has officially fallen off the deep end as he's visited by two of his former coworkers, one of which is a dwarf named Gary. Arthur murders the taller man, and he allows Gary to leave his apartment... but the door is locked, and he cannot reach the door guard by himself; he needs Arthur to unlock it for him. Besides this disturbing scene that objectifies a little person, Gary has his height made fun of a couple of times throughout the movie, and he never once stands up to the mistreatment.

A worse example is in *Cyrano (2022)* when Peter Dinklage is cast in a reimagining of the usually long-nosed vigilante. As he spends the movie singing about his love for Roxanne, he's too afraid to tell her that himself because he fears his disability would make them an incompatible pair. He never gets the chance to see his assumptions proven wrong, as he dies seconds after he and Roxanne confess their love for each other. It ultimately gives the message that little people like Cyrano are better off dead than being loved.

*****

Based on the previous section, it would be easy to conclude that Hollywood only offers an acting gig to a little person out of necessity to fit a role, and not for narrative purposes. Gladly, a few films have pushed for better intentionality behind their casting and character design decisions, which in the end ultimately paid off:

One Flew Over the Cuckoo's Nest (1975) -*United States*

Danny DeVito plays Martini, one of the mental hospital residents, who is small in stature, but his height is never acknowledged. In the scene where Randle leads a round of blackjack, Martini just gets on Randle's nerves with his sheer incomprehensibility at the game. Although a minor character, enough information comes across about Martini to raise some questions within the viewer about the ways he could've been bullied and mistreated over the years. *One Flew Over the Cuckoo's Nest* provides the subtext behind each character without being on-the-nose, while ultimately empowering multiple marginalized minority groups at once.

Shrek (2001) -*United States*

Lord Farquaad is under five feet tall, yet brags about his immense lordship over Duloc; Shrek even says upon first impression of his huge castle that Farquaad is "compensating for something." However, Shrek merely just assumed Farquaad has... something not-so-PG that's tiny. After Shrek and Donkey rescue Princess Fiona, they describe to her what she can expect from her groom-to-be by tossing around some short-related puns. These two sound like they are mocking dwarfism, but are actually mocking Fiona's overly fanciful expectations—she thought Farquaad would be a tall handsome prince. Although this still could have been an effective plot if Farquaad was of average height, adding that detail gives enough layers to his character to make an ogre (or onion) proud!

Elf (2003) - *United States*

The close of the second act introduces Miles Finch, a person with dwarfism, whose tough personality and deep, assertive voice are heard and known about before the audience even knows he's a dwarf. It's ironic—Miles Finch is supposed to be a world-famous ghost author of children's books, yet he's a big bad businessman who's as tall as a child. As the business meeting progresses, Buddy barges through the door and is the first to acknowledge Miles' height, thinking that he flew in from the North Pole. (Or maybe the South Pole.) Buddy had no intent to insult him but was simply naïve given his limited knowledge of life outside the North Pole.

Ratatouille (2007) -*United States*

The villain of this movie, Skinner, is quite short but isn't necessarily categorized under the same harmful stereotype as other short, animated villains. Exactly one minor detail is designed to point out his height: the step ladder he uses to glance out the kitchen window into the restaurant and taste test the food. Skinner doesn't belong in the kitchen, especially as its chef, because of his plan to inherit Gusteau's restaurant. In addition, his height further strengthens the brilliance of Skinner's design: with his large, round ears, his downward-pointing triangular nose, and his giant toque, he looks more like a rat than any other human, further driving the point home that he's nothing but a piece of vermin in the kitchen. That richness of his character wouldn't be as effective if Skinner were designed to be as tall as the other human characters.

Three Billboards Outside Ebbing, Missouri (2017) -*United States*

As Mildred aggressively presses the police in their search for the man who raped and murdered her daughter, an acquaintance of Mildred's, a dwarf named James, takes her out on a date. Despite being a second-hand car salesman who suffers from alcoholism, James tells her that she's still even less of a catch than he is because she can never say a nice thing to anybody nor do a nice thing for them either. Yet he did a nice thing for her by taking her out on a date because he cares about her. So bottom line: you can be a little person, but if you have no love for others, that's what will officially make you nothing.

*****

Some little people have recently called current depictions of themselves in media, "the last acceptable Blackface," because they are still getting paid to play short pop culture characters, including leprechauns, elves, Oompa Loompas, Santa's elves, and miniature versions of celebrities. In addition, "Micro Wrestling" and "Midget Boxing" both continue to be a thing, and a theme park near Kunming, China has a cutesy little village housed by "magical" dwarfs. This forces the community into a circle of victims made into clowns.

Jobs such as these could very well be the best chance for little people to get paychecks, but that just ultimately proves how broken the work economy truly is since many jobs remain inaccessible to little people. That's why you and I both must work together to change our perception of the community so that they can start being treated as fully human and fully in need of personal fulfillment in our world.

Discussion Questions

1. The film in focus, *Freaks,* rose from the ashes and finally found an audience thirty years after its original release. What do you think was the major contributing factor to its belated success?
2. How would you change the ending of *Freaks* so that it's more respectful toward the two little people and all the others in the circus? Or do you even think it needs to be changed? Why?
3. Do you think this movie is giving a good or bad image of community acceptance for little people amongst other people of average height?
4. How did you feel when you saw each of the people referred to as "freaks" in this movie? Did you feel scared? Did you feel disgusted? How does your instant reaction reflect your prejudices and attitudes toward people with physical disabilities?
5. Watch a movie from the "Disability in Film History" section. Do you agree or disagree that the movie is a negative depiction of little people? Why?
6. *One Flew Over the Cuckoo's Nest:* Do you think the film benefits from ignoring Martini's height? Would anything in the movie (say, the blackjack scene) be improved if his height was mentioned?
7. *Shrek:* Do you think that Lord Farquaad's a funny character? Why? Is it because of his height? Would any of the stuff Farquaad does still be funny if he were of average height? How would that affect the overall message of the film? Would it be better or worse?
8. *Elf:* Looking at the "angry elf" scene, who were you laughing at? Buddy or Miles Finch? Do you believe this

scene was making fun of Mr. Finch's height? Would you say that this is still a positive portrayal of little people?
9. *Ratatouille:* Imagine if Skinner were the same height as the other human characters. What would change about his character? What would change about the way he interacts with the other props and objects in the kitchen?
10. *Three Billboards Outside Ebbing, Missouri:* Whenever Peter Dinklage was on screen, did you ever laugh? At which parts? Did you feel bad for laughing? Do you think those scenes were intended to be funny?
11. Upon watching all the good examples, are there any you believe shouldn't be considered a good example?
12. Now, onto some personal takeaways. Survey all the things in your house that you routinely grab for throughout the day: the utensil drawer, the toothbrush, the knob to the front door, how high your car seat is from the ground, literally anywhere you would sit or take something off a shelf, table, etc. Now, imagine if you were somewhere between four feet and five feet tall. How would your routine change? Would your smaller legs be able to handle walking up and down the stairs as easily? How would it affect your ability to drive? What kind of assistance do you think you would need?
13. What new/surprising knowledge did you pick up from reading this chapter?
14. What's the biggest misconception you learned about the little people community?
15. And most importantly: How will you start to live differently having a new perspective on little people?

Chapter 3: Facial Disfigurement

My Personal Experience

I remember back in junior high when my school had a week dedicated to the dangers of drugs and alcohol. During a presentation that Friday, my class saw some rather traumatic images of people after near-fatal DUI accidents. One lady lost her eyes, and one lost her nose. Those horrific photos remain ingrained into my memory to this day.

Another exposure I had to people with facial disfigurement, while not too impactful, was when I volunteered at a library event hosted by a local nonprofit business intent on helping kids with disabilities. A girl there, around thirteen, had a noticeably disfigured face and needed to walk with the aid of a walker. Another typical-looking younger girl at that event, who was around six, kept running away from the older girl because she was scared of how she looked. I understood the younger girl's childish fear but did my best to talk to the older girl respectfully like I would any other kid.

Yet that brief instance hardly impacted me. If anything, I only got real long-term exposure to it through my eventual superhero obsession in my late grade school/early middle school years. Everyone knows how most of these origin stories often go: a guy either falls into toxic waste or survives a near-fatal accident, then becomes a supervillain with superpowers. Maybe sometimes he or she will become a superhero. That cool idea of deciding on a superhuman character's design made me want to draw my versions of the Batman villains, as well as my own superhero creations.

There were a lot of unnaturally ugly villains across media throughout my youth, including Batman's foes: the Joker,

Penguin, Mr. Freeze, Bane, and Two-Face (who I dressed up as for Halloween in sixth grade with a homemade costume and face paint). Although some heroes had facial disfigurements too, all of which I thought were awesome role models, especially Cyborg from *Teen Titans,* whose robot prosthetics came about after a terrible accident. I also thought the Thing from the *Fantastic Four (2005)* was cool due to his sincere desire to be human again.

And one more thing, there's a legendary quote from *SpongeBob SquarePants* that is amongst the most referenced within the fan community:

"Who ya callin' pinhead?"

Now, just for context: Patrick Star says this when he and SpongeBob are playing cowboy, and are roleplaying as two outlaws: Dirty Dan and Pinhead Larry. SpongeBob tries to give Patrick the role of "Pinhead," and Patrick says this quote while his face morphs to look like a goofy hillbilly with a bucktooth. As a kid watching, I didn't get the joke, and I doubt other kids got it either. To us, Patrick was just making another funny face. But now I realize it was a reference to "pinheads," the offensive term given to people with microcephaly.

So as a kid, I cannot say I thought low of whoever had facial disfigurement, but I would say that I didn't have sincere sympathy for those whose facial disfigurement weakened them or made them look ugly. For the most part, I would say I'm currently typical for how most would react if they saw someone who looked like a Batman villain, I'd be afraid and not want to look them in the eye.

Quick Facts

Here are some common examples of facial disfigurement:

- Acne: The most common facial disfigurement, with roughly 50 million Americans affected a year.
- Diprosopus: (Greek for "two faces.") When an infant may be born with more facial features as if the embryo during development tried to split into twins but stopped at some point. Hardly any cases live very long after birth, but one boy named Tres Johnson lived as old as thirteen!
- Facial Paralysis: When either half or all of the face loses muscle tone; over half of these treatments are untreatable and often include Bell's Palsy.
- Neurofibromatosis: When incurable, sometimes cancerous tumors grow on nerves all over the body. Type 1 shifts the bones as well, and type 2 can cause significant hearing problems.
- Microcephaly: When the baby is born with a much smaller cranium than expected.
- Macrocephaly: When the baby is born with a much larger cranium than expected.
- Proteus Syndrome: When bones, flesh, and tissue grow in asymmetrical ways. Fewer than 1 million people worldwide have this. Some cases also include other disabilities, such as vision loss or seizures.
- Treacher Collins Syndrome: When facial bones and tissues are underdeveloped.
- Traumatic injury: This includes burns, scars, or loss of body parts—one of the leading causes of disability in the US.

The Film in Focus

Title	The Elephant Man
Director	David Lynch
Writer	Eric Bergren, Christopher De Vore
Main Cast	Anthony Hopkins, John Hurt
Studio	Brooksfilms
Country	United Kingdom
Release	10 October 1980
Runtime	2 hr. 4 min.

Synopsis

Frederick Treves discovers John Merrick as a starring circus sideshow attraction in London's East End, under the name, "the Elephant Man," because of his enormous bodily growths that resemble elephant skin. Merrick's abusive owner asks Treves to analyze him at the hospital. He's inspected and then sent back, but injuries due to the owner's abuse force Merrick to the hospital once again for an extended visit.

However, the hospital heads do not want Merrick in their care, because his case cannot be cured. But Treves remains diligent; he helps Merrick mutter out some words, who in turn proves his ability to read quite well. Thus, Merrick is given temporary residence. Then after a lot of debate amongst the hospital staff, accompanied by a strong word from Queen Victoria herself, the hospital eventually gives Merrick permanent residence.

Meanwhile, a man arranges a paid crowd to break into Merrick's room to gawk at him. During this horrific night, Merrick's former circus owner kidnaps him, then locks him up inside a cage with baboons back at his old circus. The other circus acts help get

Merrick a ticket back home, and on his way there, at the train station, all the other onlookers chase him into a corner, where he desperately shouts, "I am not an animal! I am a human being!" The police escort him home, only to the news that he is dying of chronic obstructive pulmonary disease. So Treves dresses him in a nice suit for a trip to the theater, where he finally feels accepted by the crowd. That night, he lies on his bed and peacefully dies in his sleep.

The Film's Portrayal of the Disability

Fun fact: *The Elephant Man* helped create the Oscars' Best Makeup and Hairstyling category! After the 53rd Annual Academy Awards ceremony, many people sent letters of complaint to the AMPAS for ignoring Christopher Tucker's prosthetic work on John Hurt (who played Mr. Merrick), which was designed off the real casts taken directly from the real Merrick's body, so they created a new category for other similar artists to be recognized in the future.

Yet before any production work started on this motion picture, the film went through pitches from studio to studio, only to be turned down by approximately half a dozen different studios since they believed nobody wanted to "see a movie about a monster like this." Yet once a studio finally gave the feature the green light, throughout production, the crew never considered the project a "monster movie." Once the film was complete and made its world premiere, other people with conditions similar to Merrick's reported finding the courage to speak up, allowing greater growth of research programs for facial disfigurement.

But what about the case of the real John Merrick? Well, his condition began to develop at age five, then he lost his mother to bronchial pneumonia, and his new stepmother treated him cruelly. He was incapable of smiling, his spine resembled a corkscrew, his head gradually grew heavier, his speech gradually became more intelligible, and 90% of his body was affected. Also, his name wasn't John. It was Joseph. But in reminiscence papers written about him, his name was changed to "John," so this movie is a reference to that detail.

In terms of his exact case, some believed for a while that he had Neurofibromatosis until that theory was discarded in favor of Proteus Syndrome. Yet Joseph Merrick could have very well had a unique one-of-a-kind disease.

David Lynch's directorial efforts along with the rest of the crew did their best to be respectful to the humanity of Joseph Merrick but, I believe, ultimately failed. Upon Merrick's introduction scene, he is framed and lit as if introducing a monster akin to the Wolf Man or Dracula, with only his silhouette seen. Immediately, the audience is told this man is a monster and barely even human. From there, more efforts are given to further isolate him in methods that are disguised as ways of helping him. The hospital sends him to an isolation ward, and instead of helping him get a home of his own in an apartment or flat, he's given residence at the hospital, where he can be isolated further from the world.

Even worse, this involves no effort on Merrick's end; it's all served to him on a silver platter like he's a beggar on the street. He can read and think perfectly fine, his only communication drawback being his difficulty in speaking. So there's no reason for all these "charitable deeds" to be done for him when can ignite the action himself. He doesn't even do that while trapped at the circus sideshow, he needs the others there to help him escape. That in turn makes one wonder, what about those other victims at the sideshow? Shouldn't they also get out? Don't they matter too?

Then the very end happens, when Merrick gets to attend the theater and receives a standing ovation from the whole crowd. But why? The entire movie was spent having people laugh at him and run from him, and now suddenly he's one of them? This feels more like an attempt to make the audience cry with an inspirational ending, even if it doesn't make a whole lot of sense.

Now regarding the historical accuracy of the events depicted, it's not entirely true. For example, some memoirs have stated that Merrick's owner, Tom Norman (named "Bytes" in the movie), apparently treated him pretty well, only acting sadistically toward him as part of the act during live shows. This previous owner of his also did not kidnap him back, but rather it was a business partner from Austria who kidnapped him, which in turn means the scene where Merrick was left to die in a baboon cage was entirely fictional. The clear disregard for history proves a lack of respect toward the real man of focus. So no matter how much *The Elephant Man* tries its best to humanize Joseph Merrick, the emotional manipulation sadly takes priority.

The Disability in Film History

Unlike most of the other disabilities discussed throughout this book, facial disfigurement appears quite frequently in movies that a majority of the American public has heard about. Their impact has been quite undeniable as they've appeared everywhere in pop culture, with costumes worn all over on Halloween and at Comic Con events. But along with their popularity comes a dark side...

The Villain Trope

The most common cinematic representation of this disability is the many iconic villains of pop culture with physical trauma on their faces, often caused by scars or burns. These include *Nosferatu, The Phantom of the Opera, The Man Who Laughs,* Leatherface in *The Texas Chainsaw Massacre*, Jason Voorhees in *Friday the 13th*, Freddy Krueger in *A Nightmare on Elm Street*, Chuckie in *Child's Play*, Lord Voldemort in *Harry Potter*, the Joker in *Batman*, the Penguin in *Batman Returns*, Harvey Dent in *The Dark Knight*, the Red Queen in *Alice in Wonderland (2010)* and *Alice Through the Looking Glass (2016)*, Red Skull in *Captain America: The First Avenger*, Harry Osborn in *The Amazing Spider-Man 2*, Killer Croc in *Suicide Squad*, Doctor Poison in *Wonder Woman*, Raoul Silva in *Skyfall*, Blofeld in *Spectre*, Lyutsifer Safin in *No Time to Die*, and Darth Vader, Emperor Palpatine, and Supreme Leader Snoke in *Star Wars*.

The Toughness Trope

Marvel Studios has mastered this trope to make Nick Fury and Thor both look like they overcame a fatal obstacle with their eyepatches. The *Harry Potter* franchise has done a similar thing with Mad-Eye Moody, whose maniacal personality is a perfect reflection of his magical prosthetic eye. In these cases, whether they have an eyepatch or a prosthetic, these (never female, always male) characters are designed to look cool with the blaring flaws that they wear as badges of honor.

The Pity Trope

The most classic example of this is *The Hunchback of Notre Dame,* the tale of a social outcast who terrifies everyone with his appearance but eventually is accepted back into society. But a more recent example is *Wonder,* a movie designed to manipulate the audience's tears from watching a grade school boy with Treacher Collins syndrome suffer for nearly two hours. There's also *The English Patient,* where the whole plot revolves around a burn victim and the memories that led him to this condition, and for the sake of trying to make the story of his teary-eyed love affair even sadder.

The Disease Trope

Although very few cases of facial disfigurement have a cure, some movies still try to give them fantastical remedies to make the audience feel a little better. The *Pirates of the Caribbean* franchise features Will Turner's father, Bootstrap Bill, who, upon a curse to join the crew of Captain Davy Jones, mutated into the sea, complete with barnacles breaking out over his face like warts. Eventually, the curse is lifted, and he looks like a regular human being again. Also, in *District 9,* the process of Wikus turning into an alien is treated as a gross disease, with vomit and bodily wounds included. In *Hereditary,* Charlie is played by Milly Shapiro, who has Cleidocranial Dysostosis, and her grotesque appearance is there to make her look broken in comparison to her older brother, and thus, overall inferior. Such imagery as these three examples is designed to terrify the audience into associating an atypical face with a horrible disease.

The Superhuman Trope

This disability could also be featured as a side effect for ordinary people who suddenly gained superpowers. The best examples include *Spawn*, the Thing in *Fantastic Four (2005),* and *Deadpool.* Also consider Sloth in *The Goonies,* whose hideous appearance comes with his tremendous strength. In the climax, he's also framed to look like a superhero with his Superman t-shirt.

However, facial disfigurements in real life are never side effects of superhuman abilities.

The Victim Trope

A regular face gets burnt or injured, perhaps losing an eye, then suddenly life goes bad for the victim, and self-acceptance of their fate is never an option. In *Thor: Ragnarok,* Thor loses an eye, but in the next movie he's featured in, *Avengers: Infinity War,* he's given a perfect prosthetic eye before he has a chance to consider accepting his new fate. In *Nope,* there is a brief backstory of a girl who is brutally mauled by a chimpanzee, and as an adult regularly wears a veil over her disfigured face. In *Under the Skin,* the alien wearing a woman's skin lures a man with a severe facial disfigurement into her trap. Not only is this a harmful depiction of someone like him becoming a victim, but his outcast predicament also makes him weaker to the alien's seduction; not to mention he's made to look incapable of saving himself.

The Comic Relief Trope

A terrible thought indeed, that movies would take joy in making fun of people who look different, but there are still rare cases of this happening. That includes the numerous creative ways Deadpool thinks of to describe his flesh after gaining his superpowers. Then over in the Marvel Cinematic Universe, Nick Fury is introduced in *Iron Man 2,* and over the next decade, audiences are left wondering what sort of epic life-or-death fight Fury had to get out of alive to acquire his cool eyepatch, until *Captain Marvel* reveals that it was just because a cat scratched his eye. Quite anticlimactic.

And talking further about *Freaks,* the cast includes three performers with microcephaly. The most famous one, Simon

"Schlitzie" Metz, wore a dress in the film, as he did in his circus acts, and was mockingly referred to as a "she."

*****

Most films traditionally depict facial disfigurement as evil or undesirable, and this is the one disability that has the longest to go before it's widely well represented in film. But there are some movies that have utilized those familiar tropes to advance their stories while also sincerely depicting the pain behind the disability:

Braveheart (1995) - *United States*

Robert the Bruce's father has leukemia, so that means Robert shall soon carry the pressure as Scotland's next King. His father does everything in his willpower to install the proper mindset of a king as they're at war against the English, yet William Wallace's acts of terrorism on the enemies eventually reveal the king's real skewed morality; he turns into an antagonistic force against his son and ultimately becomes a leading cause for Wallace's execution. It's sad to see such an influential political power be the cause of corruption during such a dark period in Scotland's history, but Mel Gibson's iconic blockbuster triggers believable empathy behind this force: the man is dying of a fatal disease.

The Lord of the Rings (2001-2003) - *United States*

Gollum was once a carefree hobbit named Smeagol until he found the ring of Sauron, which upon immediate contact, corrupted his morality to the point he killed his best friend just to claim ownership of it. From there, he spent five hundred years inside a cave alone eating nothing but fish, which warped his body beyond recognizability. It's such a tragic story within this legendary three-part epic, but it gives an impactful case of how a bodily disfigurement can at times reflect a series of regrettable actions.

Kill Bill (2003-2004) -*United States*

Elle Driver failed in her martial arts training under the legendary martial arts master, Pai Mei, so he plucked out one of her eyes to make her notice her shortcomings. While she may have been permanently scarred from the way she let her master down, Elle turns her flaw into a badge of honor, even turning her eyepatches into fashion accessories, as if she did make her master proud after all. This two-part serial's protagonist, the Bride, eventually makes her way to Pai Mei for training, and she goes up in combat against Elle, and in the end, plucks out Elle's other eye. The Bride fulfilled Pai Mei's legacy, so walked away with honor, but Elle Driver failed his legacy, so is left to wander with a permanently disfigured appearance.

Mad Max: Fury Road (2015) -*Australia*

This wildly fantastical take on the future gives an exaggeration of what could happen if we let our current state of abusing Earth's natural resources continue. Most people in this apocalyptic wasteland are covered in severe warts, cysts, tumors, swelling, and growths, and their leader, Immortan Joe, is no exception. Across the series of wild car chases, Max and Imperator Furiosa kill the Immortan and shift the citadel's social order, opening up hope for a healthier climate in the distant future. *Mad Max: Fury Road* illustrates how the governing bodies cannot truly help the sick and wounded, since for the most part, they caused the calamity in the first place.

Us (2019) -*United States*

The son of the family in focus, Jason, always wears a monster mask on top of his head and is obsessed with perfecting a magic trick where a flame appears from snapping his fingers. Then while vacationing in Santa Cruz, the family's tethereds (or doppelgangers) arrive, and Jason's copy of himself, named Pluto, leads him into the closet. Pluto wears a scary white mask over his entire head, and Jason discovers that he can make him mirror his actions. He gets Pluto to pull back his mask, and reveal that half his face was burnt a long time ago. Pluto, like Jason, also loves fire and let his obsession permanently fracture his face. Thus, facial disfigurement plays an appropriate role in this horror-social satire to warn us of how deadly an obsession can become.

*****

The future of Hollywood is greatly dependent on the wider inclusion of the disability community, especially those whose appearance goes against the grain of beauty. Having perfect skin, hair, eyes, and teeth is such a high priority in the moviemaking business that it often means the ones cast for a role don't necessarily fit the part—they need makeup prosthetics to look closer to the part. But if a casting director opened up the possibility to those who already look the part without the need for makeup effects, it would give those kinds of people jobs throughout Hollywood, along with the long-overdue chance in the spotlight. If an average-looking person deserves a chance, why not someone who's atypical-looking?

Discussion Questions

1. The film in focus, *The Elephant Man,* has gained universal critical acclaim; at the time the book was written, this movie was #154 on IMDb's Top 250. Should it be higher on the list, lower on the list, unchanged, or not on the list at all? Why?
2. Reference back to the "Film's Portrayal of the Disability" section. How would you change *The Elephant Man* so that all the details of John Merrick's life were historically accurate? How would this change the film's portrayal of facial disfigurement? Would it be better or worse?
3. Scientists have tried to identify Merrick's case for over a hundred years but never reached a definite conclusion. Do you think there is a direct answer, or that his case truly is one-of-a-kind? Why do you think this?
4. How did you feel when you first saw John Merrick in the movie? Did you feel scared? Maybe sad? How does your instant reaction to his form reflect your prejudices and attitudes toward facial disfigurement?
5. Watch a movie from the "Disability in Film History" section. Do you agree or disagree that the movie is a negative depiction of facial disfigurement? Why?
6. *Braveheart:* Have you ever had a close friend or family member acquire a disease similar to leukemia, one that distorts the face? What did it make you think in terms of honoring the person's legacy?
7. *The Lord of the Rings:* What types of habits can you think of that cause facial disfigurement? Are these preventable, like in Smeagol's case, or are they not preventable depending on the unique circumstance?

8. *Kill Bill:* What real-life cases can you think of where someone's facial disfigurement came about as a result of preventable action? What examples came about as a result of obstacles outside the victim's control?
9. *Mad Max: Fury Road:* Does seeing the infected people in this movie disturb you or scare you out of something? What is it?
10. *Us:* Have you ever seen images of people who were permanently disfigured because of severe burns? How did it make you feel? Did it convict you of anything?
11. Upon watching all these good examples, are there any you believe shouldn't be considered a good example?
12. Now, onto some personal takeaways. Think back to a time you got a horrible zit on your face back in junior high or high school (you also could think back to when you had any sort of embarrassing flaw on your face). How did you feel about going out in public? Did others ever comment on that zit or blemish? That's a taste of how it feels for someone with facial disfigurement to be out in public, but far worse.
13. What new/surprising knowledge did you pick up from reading this chapter?
14. What's the biggest misconception you just learned about the community of people with facial disfigurement?
15. And most importantly: How will you start to live differently having a new perspective on those with facial disfigurement.

Chapter 4: Autism

My Personal Experience

At age two, my parents noticed that I had a speech delay, so they took me to weekly language therapy sessions until I was around five years old. At that time, I always preferred to do things on my own, particularly puzzles, which kept me occupied for hours. I got angry and threw a fit if something unpredictable came up outside the preplanned schedule, which only got worse when I reached Kindergarten.

While I had basic social skills such as eye contact, more advanced cues such as another's subtle signs of emotion I could not pick up on. So Kindergarten was when I started spending an hour away from the regular class time to learn appropriate behavior skills with a special education teacher. Right as I started first grade, my parents took me to the University of Washington's Autism Center, where I was diagnosed with PDD-NOS (Pervasive Developmental Disorder – Not Otherwise Specified).

At the time, I never had a second thought as to why I was taking language therapy, nor why I had to take time outside the classroom for special education learning. Although I did notice my inactive social life compared to my sister. Like other neurotypical girls, she always had friends over, especially at her birthday parties, but I seldom got invited over to someone else's house, and consistent friendships where I would invite those same people over were nearly nonexistent. Heck, for two of my birthdays in a row, I just invited all the boys from my class rather than any specific friends.

I have no recollection of even hearing the word "autism" until I think later into my grade school years. But I still didn't understand what that meant until high school—the worst years of my life. Every teenager almost seems to be a professional at being insecure about themselves, so imagine that same scenario with an autistic teenager believing he is pretty much incomplete. That insecurity, coupled with trying to make friends without any idea what friendship is, made for some painful memories.

Now, it's important to know that there's a common saying within the autism community: "If you've met one person with autism, you've met one person with autism." That means the autistic traits of one person are completely different than the autistic traits of another; everybody who falls on the spectrum has different sensory needs, it's not one-size-fits-all.

For example, many people on the spectrum can't stand being touched—they describe it as feeling like their skin is peeled off. However, I have no problem with being touched, and love giving and receiving hugs! Yet I have a noticeable speech delay and need some time to put my thoughts into words; it gets harder for me to do so when I'm nervous or afraid. Yet I've known others on the spectrum who had the opposite problem: they were always talking and never knew when to shut up! They actually talked more when they were nervous or afraid! So people with autism are just like other people: their personalities can't be categorized because they are just as varied as neurotypicals.

I hope for other autistic kids to build healthy long-lasting friendships earlier than I did, and with the right skills necessary. It's key to see the core essentials of what makes autism what it is, so on the next page are some important statistics. Bear in mind that these facts are ones even I didn't know before doing my research.

Quick Facts

The Centers for Disease Control and Prevention defines Autism Spectrum Disorder (ASD) as, "a developmental disability characterized by persistent impairments in social interaction and the presence of restricted, repetitive patterns of behaviors, interests, or activities."

There are five types of disorders on the autism spectrum:

- <u>Asperger's:</u> Since 2013 it's been called Level 1 Autism Disorder.
- <u>Childhood Disintegrative Disorder (CDD):</u> At about age three, the child shows delays in speech and behavior.
- <u>Kanner's Syndrome:</u> Discovered in 1943 by psychiatrist Leo Kanner of John Hopkins University.
- <u>Pervasive Developmental Disorder – Not Otherwise Specified (PDD-NOS):</u> A mild type of autism with a range of symptoms.
- <u>Rett Syndrome:</u> A condition more common in girls that is detectable right at infancy.

Among other statistics:

- About 1.85% of children have been identified with ASD.
- 86%-91% of US citizens have adequate knowledge of ASD.
- 35% of people aged 19-23 with ASD have no job or education after high school.
- In 2018, it was estimated that families impacted by autism are 84% less likely to attend a church.
- In 2009, it was estimated that 163,000 U.S. children with ASD were living below the poverty line.
- 19% of young adults with ASD have ever lived independently from their parents.

The Film in Focus

Title	Rain Man
Director	Barry Levinson
Writer	Ronald Bass, Barry Morrow
Main Cast	Tom Cruise, Dustin Hoffman
Studio	United Artists
Country	United States
Release	16 December 1988
Runtime	2 hr. 13 min.

Synopsis

Charlie Babbitt, a selfish car dealer, just got half of his deceased father's fortune. Except the other half went to his autistic brother named Raymond, a brother he didn't even know he had until that very moment. Even worse, Raymond will never spend that money because he has no understanding of money. So Charlie decides to get his brother's money by taking him from Cincinnati to Los Angeles… by car… because Raymond is too afraid of airplanes.

The extra-long road trip throws in many bumps to challenge Charlie's patience, particularly Raymond's refusal to go outside while it's raining. Charlie also discovers Raymond's brilliant mind: he can count toothpicks in a second, perform impossibly complicated math in his head, and keep track of where every card is on a poker table. When they make it to LA, Charlie tries to convince a psychiatrist that he should have custody of his brother. Yet after the psychiatrist proves that Raymond can't make decisions, they decide he should stay in the institution back in Cincinnati. Before saying goodbye, Charlie tells Raymond he loves having him as a brother.

The Film's Portrayal of the Disability

Rain Man was inspired by Kim Peek, a man with savant syndrome and macrocephaly who could memorize entire books after reading or hearing them exactly once, even memorizing the Bible cover to cover at age seven. He also spoke at panels where people asked him obscure historical questions, all of which he immediately knew the answer to. Dustin Hoffman spent a lot of time with Peek to prepare for his role.

In an interview shortly after the film's release, Dustin Hoffman referred to autism as a "terrible disease," even saying he felt everyone had a degree of being autistic, the same way one would have a degree of being a killer. Movie critics Siskel and Ebert also called autism a disease while reviewing the movie on their show, describing Raymond as a character who can never change. This proves how little people at the time knew about Autism Spectrum Disorders. But that doesn't mean the people behind the movie didn't try their best to depict it with the resources they had available, even to the extent of casting real people with autism, Asperger's, and Down Syndrome to populate the institution Raymond lives at.

As one with autism, I can say that *Rain Man* gets almost everything right in depicting the disability. Raymond has peculiar, strange motivations behind his thought process, his most noticeable being his sense of security found in strict routine; he wants maple syrup on the table before the pancakes at breakfast arrive, and needs the furniture in specific positions at every hotel. If one thing in his schedule is out of line, even his TV shows, he becomes terrified. He also has peculiar hobbies involved with numbers and structure, such as memorizing the phone book and drawing buildings from memory.

Unfortunately, his other irrational fears get in his way, more so his brother's way. In a major pivotal scene, he expresses his fear of flying on any airline that has any history of crashes, and in another, the police sirens at night make him reluctant to even go inside his brother's car to drive past them.

At times he seems to lack common sense, such as stopping in the middle of the crosswalk when the "walk" signal changes to "don't walk," or only wearing underwear from K-Mart. He has such a perplexing mind that it's hard to know what he's thinking, or even if he's thinking at all. Thus, he seems unable to hear someone calling to him unless he's comfortable around them.

In addition to his delay in responding, Raymond answers questions from a half-hour ago and doesn't react to hearing about his father's death. Although the film's logic about the way Raymond thinks isn't realistic, people with autism always are thinking of something, just like anyone not on the spectrum. They can listen and mourn in the same capacity as their peers.

Raymond's mind is so brilliant that Charlie thinks he should work for NASA, but that possibility is quickly chucked out the window when Raymond says he thinks both a candy bar and a car cost the same. It's a part of the film's dated mindset that people "suffering" from the "disease" that is autism cannot live successful lives, even the doctor refers to him as a "retarded, high functioning savant." Back then, the word "retard" was simply a diagnosis, but nowadays, it's considered an insult.

Besides the political incorrectness, *Rain Man* is brimming with more dehumanizing depictions of autism. That includes Raymond's inability to distinguish between two different decisions, and that includes the reason he was separated from

Charlie in the first place. The mere sight of hot water is enough to bring back Raymond's painful memory of when he was sent away because he burned Charlie while bathing him, making him look like a danger to himself and everyone around him.

So while *Rain Man* is a reflection of the time it was made, it's better to realize that this proves how far we've come in understanding Autism Spectrum Disorders. Back then, an autism diagnosis was reserved only for children with severe developmental delays; many researchers back then believed only 4-5 out of every 10,000 children had autism. Now there are many better resources to help people understand themselves and know what kind of help they need. So is *Rain Man* a great movie to get to know autism? Well, the answer is both yes and no.

The Disability in Film History

As I was looking up movies that feature autism, almost all of them were made after *Rain Man*. Whether that particular film was the reason more movies with autism started getting made, I wouldn't know, but I can certainly say the way it depicts autism and Asperger's is ever-present in almost all films after it that feature the disability, whether to enhance the story arc of a non-autistic character or to be a challenge for the autistic character.

The Burden Trope

The most common of these depictions is autistic people being treated as burdens. The 1992 adaptation of the classic novel, *Of Mice and Men,* makes Lennie out to be not only incapable of independence, but also not good at anything. His one strength, that being his physical strength, is only proven to be dangerous, even deadly, and George's course of action is to put his brother out of his misery. This hopeless ending skews any artistic purpose the novel may have had and instead unintentionally suggests that people like Lennie are better off dead.

This kind of treatment happens as well in *What's Eating Gilbert Grape,* Arnie Grape is constantly giggling in his own little world and is often seen climbing up the town's water tower. No matter how many times the cops have to stop him, he never learns his lesson. His mother calls him "helpless," and his brother wants to get him a new brain, so not even his dysfunctional family respects him. Rarely is Arnie ever seen as fully human, he's just an annoying burden to the whole family.

The Fetish Trope

The next most common trait is when autism is used just to manipulate a romantic plot, such as Daniel's Asperger's in *P.S. I Love You.* He has rather poor communication skills in the way he's awfully blunt and often just flat-out rude, yet his letters written to the main woman in the film, Holly, make him plenty enough of a catch. Unfortunately, without autism in the mix, this would be just another standard romantic drama.

The Emotional Manipulation Trope

Extremely Loud and Incredibly Close has been widely considered one of if not the worst movie to ever get an Academy Award nomination for Best Picture. The main boy, coincidentally named Oskar, is suggested in one scene to potentially have Asperger's, even though in the original book this movie was based on, he was never said to have it. Along with this, the suspicion of him having Asperger's is tied with the mere fact that he's a genius because apparently, autistic=smart. This is an entirely false stereotype about ASD.

The Disease Trope

For the longest time, people have believed autism was a disease. Even to this day, some people still think that it's a preventable condition caused by ludicrous things like drinking or vaccines. Movies at times reflect that assumption. In *The Lighthouse of the Orcas,* the boy in the movie never speaks and is unable to form a connection with anything besides orcas. His mother moves them to the seashore so he could connect with the orcas and potentially be cured of his shut-in condition. In the end, he is assumed to be on a path to remedy this when he finally mutters some sound out of his mouth. This is just one example of filmmakers using autism for the dramatic effect of making the audience cheer when someone finally becomes "normal."

The Inspiration Trope

I Am Sam attempts to show an autistic character standing up against all odds to do the impossible, but fails. The man named Sam is stuck raising his daughter single-handedly but then must fight for custody of her when he was deemed unable to raise her because he has the mentality of a seven-year-old. This feel-good courtroom drama does more harm than good in the representation of autism because along with taking advantage of the disability to raise sympathy for the hero, it also gets the facts wrong. Essentially, the movie says that autism is a measure of IQ, which is entirely false and doesn't present any evidence to support that assumption. So with a skewed perspective of what autism is really like, this movie is an ugly example of exploiting the disability just to win over audiences.

The Superhuman Trope

Other instances of autism in movies have used it for the sake of making a more "superhuman" character, whether it's a hero made into an expert fighter or a supervillain made into more of a threat. In *The Accountant (2016)*, Ben Affleck's character, Christian, is somewhere in the middle of these two. He uses his brilliant mind with numbers to perform criminal heists from an organization. He may be the main character, but Christian is still a crook... not a good image for the autism community!

The "Other" Trope

In *Power Rangers*, the Blue Ranger is on the autism spectrum, and this just contributes to him being a part of these other "misfits" who aren't made to belong in society; they just go off into a corner away from everybody else. Or for a better example, there's *The Boy Who Could Fly*, which depicts a boy with autism as if he's something magical or fairytale-like. Both of these scenarios are designed to associate ASD with not belonging in the real world, or like their unique traits are merely ingredients to creating quirky heartwarming characters.

The Comic Relief Trope

In *There's Something About Mary*, Mary's brother has a clear developmental disorder, even if it's not explicitly addressed as autism or Asperger's. There are numerous occasions when he tackles whoever touches his ears, and only for the sake of really unfunny slapstick. And while this Disney classic also doesn't explicitly mention autism, being it's a film about animals, *The Lion King (1994)* features a hyena named Ed who shows some autistic stereotypes. That includes constant laughing, an inability to speak, heightened stupidity compared to the other hyenas, and a face that looks more... skewed than the others. Top that off with the label of him being among the villains, and kids watching are subliminally being told that kids who do things like Ed are best to be avoided, or even worse, bullied.

*****

There isn't as much cinematic representation of the autism community as there is for the other disabilities in this book, but there are great hidden gems which portray autism respectfully:

Mary and Max (2009) -*Australia*

Max is a lonely obese man who has trouble sleeping, gets anxiety attacks, can't understand nonverbal signs, thinks people are very confusing, goes out in public wearing a helmet, earplugs, and nose plugs, can read two pages at the same time, has a craving for chocolate hot dogs, has an invisible friend named Mr. Ravioli, and has no real-life friends. But when he starts writing back and forth with an Australian girl named Mary, he had made a meaningful connection with someone at last. While a rather sad and bleak story, this stop motion animated gem still gives a compelling look at loneliness, insecurity, and how life-changing a friendship can be, especially to someone with ASD.

My Name is Khan (2010) -*India*

Khan, a Muslim-American who has Asperger's, seems to be getting along well when he marries a single Hindu mother... but then 9/11 happens. During that ugly period of racial prejudice against Muslims, Khan's stepson is beaten to death by bullies. To gain his devastated wife's forgiveness, he takes her exaggerated request literally: to find the president and say to him, "My name is Khan, and I am not a terrorist!" This haunting, often funny feature closes gaps of hatred using this underdog hero, not despite his Asperger's as an obstacle, but because of it as a gift.

Simple Simon (2010) -*Sweden*

Simon displays many familiar quirks of Asperger's: every one of his activities is scheduled on a pinwheel chart, he refuses to let the daily meal pattern ever break, he references an emotion reading chart to know how people are feeling, and he avoids friendships because they only give him problems beyond his comprehension. While on the search for a new girlfriend for his brother, he admits that he fears his brother could be 93.7 times better than him, yet what he finds is more than what he expected. This quirky movie faithfully portrays ASD yet also proves it's not impossible for someone on the spectrum to learn about love.

Barfi! (2012) -*India*

In the time *Barfi!* takes place, autism is considered a disease, so the film's autistic character, Jhilmil, lives a sad existence where her parents are ashamed of her. After meeting Barfi, a young deaf man, the two build a powerful bond together; she at first limits physical contact with him, but gradually becomes more comfortable having him touch her. For all she does, Jhilmil proves herself independently active to the point of a healthy romance with someone who's not ashamed of her, making this a film empowering to women, people of color, and the disability community all at once!

Life, Animated (2016) -*United States*

In his toddler years, Owen Suskind was stuck inside a shell because of his speech delay, and that was where his collection of Disney VHS tapes played a vital role. From watching the movies over and over, he began quoting them around his family, which encouraged them to build conversations made of Disney quotes to teach him how to speak. Besides giving him a voice, these films eventually spoke much more deeply to him as he got older, as when everything around him was always changing, the familiar movies gave him some comfort. Not only is this documentary a touching educational tool about the disorder, but also tells a powerful real-life coming-of-age story that even those without autism can relate to.

*****

You could watch any one of these five movies and they still wouldn't be enough for you to know the basic image of autism. In total truth, this is one of those disabilities that has such a wide range of traits that anyone of any set of skills could have it. What many called the late nineties "epidemic" of autism was in actuality not so, but rather a result of better resources made available for children to be diagnosed. In 1997, 1 out of 2,500 children received an autism diagnosis, while in 2017, 1 out of 68 received one.

The spectrum is so wide that even the student sitting next to you in class could be autistic and you wouldn't even know it. Heck, even he or she may not know it! So I'd like for you to learn the dangers of stereotyping autism; it's not a measure of intelligence, but rather a different way of thinking and observing.

Discussion Questions

1. The film in focus, *Rain Man,* won the Academy Award for Best Picture of its year. Do you agree with its win? Why or why not? What should have won?
2. How would you change the ending of *Rain Man* so that Raymond changes and goes to live with his brother? How would this alternate ending change the film's portrayal of autism? Would it be better, worse, or unchanged?
3. Looking at the types of autism at the start of this chapter, which one do you think Raymond has? What evidence makes you reach that conclusion? How does that specific categorization of ASD affect the treatment of his character?
4. From your experience, is this a realistic depiction of autism? What do you think could have been changed to make Raymond more accurate to ASD?
5. Watch a movie from the "Disability in Film History" section. Do you agree or disagree that the movie is a negative depiction of autism? Why?
6. *Mary and Max:* Do you have any friends who land on the autism spectrum? How has that friendship impacted you? Or if you have autism, how have your past friendships impacted you? How in that same way has Max been impacted by his friendship with Mary?
7. *My Name is Khan:* What does Khan do about the chaos erupted in his family after the 9/11 attacks? What does Khan's journey tell you about the worth someone with ASD has in helping society function?
8. *Simple Simon:* If you've ever had a romantic relationship, or are currently in one, consider how you picked up the "rules" of dating and compatibility. Who taught you

those rules? How do you think someone with autism would be able to pick up those rules?
9. *Barfi!:* At what point between Shruti and Barfi's relationship does Shruti get comfortable with being closer to him? If you've interacted with someone on the autism spectrum before, how comfortable with you do you think he or she was? What caused any discomfort he or she might have had?
10. *Life, Animated:* What subject are you the most obsessed about? How has that helped your personal development? How does that affect your understanding of people with autism learning how to do things like talk or pick up social skills?
11. Upon watching all these good examples, are there any you believe shouldn't be considered a good example?
12. Now, onto some personal takeaways. Next time you watch a movie, write down how many times you shift around in your seat due to feeling a bit uncomfortable, or readjust the image/volume, basically any time your focus on the film is lost because of some discomfort or inconvenience. That's how it's like for a lot of people with autism trying to watch a movie. How does this change the way you view other autistic people?
13. What new/surprising knowledge did you pick up from reading this chapter?
14. What's the biggest misconception you just learned about the ASD community?
15. And most importantly: How will you start to live differently having a new perspective on the ASD community?

Chapter 5: Limb Loss/Difference

My Personal Experience

My earliest impression of limb amputation was Captain Hook from Disney's *Peter Pan,* which I believe I first watched when I was about three years old. At the time, it didn't register to me that the character of Captain Hook was subliminally associating hand amputees as being evil, but it certainly gave me the impression that I should be reviled and frightened of whoever doesn't have a certain part of their body. Sure enough, those same types of villains having weapons for hands were everywhere throughout my childhood, many of which will be talked about more in this chapter.

There weren't a whole lot of morally good amputees in the movies and TV shows I watched, but one of the few morally good ones included Wilt from the Cartoon Network series *Foster's Home for Imaginary Friends,* who had a stub where his left arm should be. It did freak me out a little to see his arm was missing, but that shock didn't last long for me. Although he had one arm, his disability rarely came up; rather, his entire character was about being an unusually polite soul who loves basketball.

Another amputee character (although more of a stretch) from my childhood was Cyborg from *Teen Titans;* both of his arms and both of his legs were replaced with robotic body parts, and he could turn each of those limbs into weapons. While it was a little unsettling for me to see his right arm turn into a cannon, I overall thought he was a cool guy with lots of humanity.

Then again, Wilt was a tall red creature made even weirder by his disproportionate appearance, and Cyborg was half-robot, associating amputees wearing prostheses with being superhuman, so neither of these are the ideal representation of disability in children's media. However, it's still better than making either of them bad guys. But it was *Extreme Makeover: Home Edition* that became a milestone in my understanding of the humanity behind amputees, as my intro chapter described.

In talking about life outside what I saw on TV, my exposure to anybody without certain limbs is far and few in-between. One of those examples includes a girl in my elementary school who had only four fingers on her left hand— I was so shocked when I first saw her pinky-less hand! Yet that was in my younger years when people who looked different in body shape were terrifying to me. Nowadays, I can handle it.

There was another time in high school when my drama club set up a summer garage sale at my house, and an amputee woman came to buy some stuff. None of us, including myself, treated her any different or acknowledged her limitation, to us, she was simply another customer. Also, I've heard stories about people at my church whose parents had to get their legs amputated for several reasons.

My instances of meeting people without various limbs are limited to instances such as that along with the occasional time I would see somebody on the street using a wheelchair because they have only one leg. But one important thing I could certainly say is how much of a phobia it was for me to see other people who had some sort of physical disability, whether it was facial disfigurement or loss of limbs. I would avoid looking at them and going to places they most likely would be. My young childish self even thought that they were monsters.

Quick Facts

The types of amputation include:

- Congenital: When a portion of the body is either missing or incomplete from birth.
- Surgical: When direct hospital interference must remove a portion of the body if it cannot be healed.
- Traumatic: When a severe accident directly cuts off the limb, which accounts for 45% of amputee cases.

Syndromes and diseases that cause limb difference include:

- Amniotic Band Syndrome: When fibrous bands inside a mother's uterus wrap around an unborn child's limbs and fingers.
- Caudal Regression Syndrome: When the lower half of the body is underdeveloped upon birth.
- Hanhart Syndrome: When the fingers, toes, or limbs are underdeveloped at birth. The tongue or jaw may also be underdeveloped.
- TAR Syndrome: When a person is born without a radius bone in their arms.
- Vascular Disease: This causes several conditions such as aneurysms, blood clots, or varicose veins, 54% of all limb difference cases are affected by vascular disease.

Some other reasons for limb amputation:

- Birth Defects
- Cancer
- Diabetes
- Infection
- Poor Blood Circulation

- Serious Injury
- Tissue Damage

Types of artificial limbs:

- <u>Transradial Prosthesis:</u> Replaces the part of the arm missing from below the elbow.
- <u>Transhumeral Prosthesis:</u> Replaces the part of the arm missing from above the elbow.
- <u>Transtibial Prosthesis:</u> Replaces the part of the leg missing from below the knee.
- <u>Transfemoral Prosthesis:</u> Replaces the part of the leg missing from above the knee.

Other essential facts:

- Over 2 million people in the United States live with an amputation, and 28 million more are at risk of amputation.
- The Centers for Disease Control and Prevention (CDC) estimates that each year, 1,900 babies in the United States are born with an upper or lower limb difference (or both).
- Healthcare costs for amputees are about $150,000 more expensive than for non-amputees.
- The cost of a prosthetic can cost anywhere between $3,000 and $50,000.
- About 36% of amputees live with depression.
- Lower limb amputation is more common than upper limb amputation, with their percentages being 65% and 35% respectively.
- 3-D printed prostheses have lately revolutionized the industry, especially when making them for children.

The Film in Focus

Title	Forrest Gump
Director	Robert Zemeckis
Writer	Eric Roth
Main Cast	Tom Hanks, Robin Wright
Studio	Paramount Pictures
Country	United States
Release	6 July 1994
Runtime	2 hr. 22 min.

Synopsis

Forrest Gump, a man with a low-IQ, goes through many major experiences in life, from being a college football star to fighting in the Vietnam War to competing in ping pong competitions against China to running a shrimping business. During that time, his childhood best friend Jenny experiences the worst in life with her involvement in sex and drugs. There are also two other people he meets who leave an immense impact on him: Lieutenant Dan Taylor and Benjamin Buford Blue ("Bubba").

Bubba is the one who invites Forrest to join his shrimping business before his death as they're fighting together in Vietnam, and Lt. Dan had hoped to die with honor while leading his war platoon, but instead is rescued by Forrest during an ambush and later has his legs amputated. For years, Dan falls into a pitiful state as a double amputee in a wheelchair, living off the government in New York City. But once Forrest starts to run Bubba's shrimping business, Dan volunteers himself for the job as Forrest's right-hand man. During their time in the shrimping boat, Dan finds his inner peace as an amputee. Lt. Dan continues to run the shrimping business, and Forrest goes off on his own to care for his deceased mother's home.

Years later, Jenny comes back to Forrest and finally agrees to marry him, mainly because she's dying of an unknown virus and needs him to care for their son, whom she's given birth to after a time the two of them made love. At the wedding, Forrest meets a familiar face: Lt. Dan... with a new pair of prosthetic legs! He finally has his life together, and even has a fiancé. However, Jenny keeps getting sicker until she ultimately dies, leaving Forrest to joyfully raise Forrest Jr. by himself.

The Film's Portrayal of the Disability

Forrest Gump left such a powerful impression on audiences of all ages when it came out because it showed a man with a developmental disorder who experienced all the horrors of the 1950s-1980s first-hand and still came out of it just as loving and humble as he was before.

It's a massive contrast from not only Jenny, whom most fans of the movie often compare Forrest to, but also Lt. Dan, who was so horrifically traumatized by his failure in the Vietnam War that his life after his service fell to shambles as a double amputee. If it weren't for Forrest's optimism and straight thinking, Dan would never have gotten himself back up to walk toward a brighter future than what he originally planned for himself.

Though what made Lt. Dan so impactful not just on audiences, but cinema overall, was the groundbreaking digital effects used to remove his legs. In this first-ever use of CGI to remove body parts, Industrial Light and Magic had Gary Sinise wear blue stockings so they could be painted over digitally; parts of the set were likewise manipulated for his legs to maneuver around freely, and then digitally painted over to better sell the illusion that his legs were gone.

What makes Lt. Dan much more complex as a character is the conflict in his emotions; he holds a grudge against Forrest for ruining his plans to die, but will still defend Forrest whenever someone calls him stupid. He's one of the only people who recognizes that Forrest is smarter than others give him credit for... even Jenny couldn't recognize that. Aside from having mixed feelings about Forrest, Dan has the existential problems that come with being a PTSD-stricken veteran with a disability.

While living in New York City, he always slouches in a wheelchair, depends on the government to provide for him, and has toyed around with the concept of Christianity. One problem though is how he takes offense to the promise that one day he'll "walk beside Him in the kingdom of Heaven," because his condition would then prove that God isn't listening. His existence in the city that never sleeps is indeed his lowest point, but once he joins Forrest in the business of shrimping, he becomes much more optimistic in light of this new career opportunity.

He still fears that God is absent until Hurricane Carmen shows up while they're at sea, and it suddenly makes the shrimping process easy for them. Once things start to go well, Lt. Dan finally makes peace with his condition, even admitting to Forrest that he never thanked him for saving his life. Now, this part always baffled me—why did Lt. Dan admit to not having thanked Forrest but then didn't actually thank him? I believe what Dan means is that he'll no longer dwell on the past, but will acknowledge it as he commits to fixing his gaze on what lies ahead. That means he won't hold a grudge against Forrest or feel pressure to make it up to him, because the best way to thank Forrest is to live his best life possible, with or without his legs.

However, this is still one of those crowd-pleasing movies that's beloved by many but scorned by others. On the subject of disability representation, the use of Forrest's leg braces is unrealistic. He shouldn't have been able to break out of his braces so easily by just running from bullies, and never at any time in his life from there does he ever display a hint of back problems. It gives the unrealistic belief that kids who have this type of issue can be cured if they just believe hard enough.

Second, when Forrest says he knows what it's like to be in Lt. Dan's predicament of not being able to use his legs, it's in actuality pretty disrespectful. Dan presumedly never knew that Forrest had to wear braces as a child, which is nothing like having legs amputated. Forrest could at least walk with his own physical feet, Lt. Dan can't enjoy that privilege.

While those two details in the treatment of his braces are rather minor, the representation of disability in *Forrest Gump* otherwise embraces how horrifying it can be. Forrest is bullied throughout his whole life, and even his only childhood friend, Jenny, takes advantage of him. Lt. Dan's made disabled by force and gets called mean names, but still acquires prosthetic legs and even finds a wife. There's a greater promise of him leading an impactful legacy than if he let himself die in Vietnam. I guarantee that both disabled and nondisabled audiences will find something of value in this wonderful classic, especially with the reality that anyone could become disabled at any minute.

The Disability in Film History

Amputees have been used to create all sorts of convincing special effects shots, be it a soldier in a fight scene or a legless boy playing E.T., but filmmakers found other ways to dehumanize the disability.

The Villain Trope

This includes Captain Hook in *Peter Pan*, Long John Silver in *Treasure Island*, Dr. Julius No in *Dr. No*, Darth Vader in *Star Wars*, Darth Maul in *Solo: A Star Wars Story*, Klaue in the Marvel Cinematic Universe, Peter Pettigrew in *Harry Potter*, Gazelle in the *Kingsman* series, the fireys in *Labyrinth*, Candyman in *Candyman*, Big Louie in *UHF*, Dr. Claw in *Inspector Gadget*, Dr. Loveless in *Wild Wild West*, Bullet-Tooth Tony in *Snatch (2000)*, The Underminer in *The Incredibles*, Dr. Curtis Connors in *The Amazing Spider-Man*, Wallace Keefe in *Batman v. Superman: Dawn of Justice*, Donald Pierce in *Logan (2017)*, Clyde in *Logan Lucky*, and Mr. Strickland in *The Shape of Water*.

The Obstacle Trope

The loss of legs has been used in *Mary and Max* to get in the way of Mary's agoraphobic neighbor, who lost both of his legs in a war. Yet on the more inspirational side of the trope, *Soul Surfer* tells the true story of Bethany Hamilton, a woman who became a motivational spokesperson after a shark attack took her arm. Furthermore, the *How to Train Your Dragon* series has Hiccup losing his foot and Toothless the dragon losing part of his tailfin, so Hiccup builds custom prosthetic pieces for both of them, which means well but demeans their conditions to be mere plot devices that motivate their desire to improve themselves.

The Victim Trope

Toy Story has Buzz Lightyear losing his arm and *Toy Story 2* has Woody's arm getting ripped off, and both scenarios ultimately give the impression that amputees belong in the trash. On a similar note, *The English Patient* features Willem Dafoe's character losing his thumbs, and he never accepts his condition, he just complains. That victimization has also been used to hammer in audience manipulation; in *Schindler's List*, a one-armed Jew is shot dead moments after thanking Oskar Schindler for giving him work; in *Who Framed Roger Rabbit* Judge Doom uses the empty sleeve of a soldier amputee as a chalkboard eraser.

The Horror Trope

It happened when Freddy Krueger sliced off his fingers to terrify his victims in *A Nightmare on Elm Street*. It happened when Gollum bit Frodo's finger off in *The Lord of the Rings: The Return of the King* to obtain the ring. It happened when Christian Bale chopped off the finger of a man who looks exactly like him in *The Prestige* to help with his magical stage illusion. It happened (sort of) in *Thor: The Dark World* when Loki and Thor put on an act to fool the dark elves. It even happened when people without arms or legs were put on display to frighten the audience in *Freaks*.

The Violence Trope

This sort of thing is everywhere in majorly popular movies loved by lots of younger men. That includes the two *Kill Bill* movies and the entire *Saw* franchise, both of which dedicated themselves to the many creative ways they can brutally murder victims. Even historical epics such as *Braveheart, The Lord of the Rings,* and

The Revenant, as well as smaller character-driven films such as *Let Him Go* and *The Banshees of Inisherin,* have lingered on the gruesome mayhem that showcased arms, legs, and fingers getting cut off.

The Toughness Trope

127 Hours upon its release shocked the world by presenting a standard of manhood where one achieved the impossible against mother nature. Pixar used this tactic as well to make two different father figures appear tougher: Merida's dad in *Brave* and Giulia's dad in *Luca.* This also includes Captain Ahab in *Moby Dick,* Ash in the *Evil Dead* series, Mad-Eye Moody in the *Harry Potter* series, and the Winter Soldier in the Marvel Cinematic Universe. This is even used to make female characters more masculine—in *Mad Max: Fury Road,* Imperator Furiosa's robotic hand makes her fit for this action-heavy blockbuster.

The Comic Relief Trope

This includes the famous "it's just a flesh wound" scene in *Monty Python and the Holy Grail,* the two *Deadpool* movies, and the cartoonish chopping off of a guy's four fingers in *The Grand Budapest Hotel.* It's not just limited to R-rated movies, *The Addams Family (1991)* does this when Pugsly and Wednesday Addams were in their school play, and *Shrek* does this when the Gingerbread Man's legs are broken off.

The Worthlessness Trope

Johnny Got His Gun has left the main victim without his limbs, voice, vision, and hearing, his only options being a carnival act or dying. Worse still, *The Ballad of Buster Scruggs* features a man profiting from an actor without arms or legs, until he discovers he can earn more money with a chicken. So he rids himself of the limbless man by chucking him into a creek. Though neither of these examples are more dangerous than in *Million Dollar Baby* when the ultimate fate of Maggie directly says that people in her state are better off dead.

*****

Yet there are some films that portray amputees well:

The Best Years of Our Lives (1946) -*United States*

Three soldiers return from war, including a double hand amputee named Homer who now wears hook prosthetics. He particularly fears what Wilma, the woman he hopes to marry, will think of him now... would she marry a man in his condition? Starring a real WWII veteran/double amputee named Harold Russell, *The Best Years of Our Lives* gives the grim reality of soldiers after their service, while still providing some hope despite their scars.

Moonstruck (1987) -*United States*

After Ronny's left hand got chopped up, his fiancé at the time left him, now he constantly compares himself to his perfect brother Johnny. Thus, he benefits from meeting Loretta, whom Johnny just got engaged to, and she tells Ronny that his fiancé only left him because she was a snare to him. This genius romantic comedy offers among the wisest treatment of limb loss ever seen, as the script hardly ever brings up Ronny's disability.

Saving Private Ryan (1998) -*United States*

Somewhere between twenty and thirty real amputees and paraplegics were brought in to film the iconic Omaha Beach sequence, and the results are horrifying. Steven Spielberg's successful WWII epic became one of the most important war movies ever because the narrative never sugarcoated the brutality behind the soldiers who gave their lives.

Finders Keepers (2015) -*United States*

Amputee John Wood made the strange decision to keep his foot, and Shannon Whisnant somehow got the embalmed limb after buying a grill from John. Shannon sees the discovery as his lucky break into fame, but John wants his foot back, for it memorializes his father after he died in the same plane crash which left him an amputee. Yet after his trial against Shannon, he learns to overcome his survivor's guilt and become his own man.

In This Corner of the World (2016) -*Japan*

Once the atomic bomb drops on Hiroshima, the impact kills the little sister of Suzu, who was holding onto her sister's hand with her right hand, which she lost along with her sister. Suzu now blames herself for her sister's death, and she lost the hand she used to paint and draw with. Such a tragic existence of a girl forever hurt by war utilizes limb loss not to force sympathy, but to prove the destructive powers of war as they put indescribable guilt onto the next generation.

*****

Just when you think you know as much as you can about this difficult subject of amputees and the lives they live, there's always a whole new world's worth of information you never thought was there. So, a suitable place to start in familiarizing yourself with their struggle is thinking critically about the entertainment you watch.

Discussion Questions

1. The film in focus, *Forrest Gump,* was the highest-grossing film of its year and won the Oscar for Best Picture. Why do you think that audiences and critics alike fell in love with this movie? Did its use of disability have anything to do with it?
2. What if Lt. Dan was left to die in Vietnam like his ancestors? How would the events of Forrest's life be different? Or if he lived, what if he got to keep his legs? What would have changed in the plot if he could physically walk through it all?
3. Would you say Lt. Dan is an inspirational character? Does his disability have anything to do with his inspirational prowess? How about Forrest Gump? Is he an inspiration just because of his low IQ?
4. Do you think Jenny was just taking advantage of Forrest's disability? Or do you think her love for him was genuine? What details from the movie make you think that?
5. Watch a movie from the "Disability in Film History" section. Do you agree or disagree that the movie is a negative depiction of limb loss or limb difference? Why?
6. *The Best Years of Our Lives:* Do you think there's ever an instance when the treatment of Homer's condition feels manipulative toward the audience's emotions? If so, how would you change the ending so that it doesn't fall into that trap?
7. *Moonstruck:* Did a traumatic event ever happen to you that you blamed a member of the family on? How was Loretta a needed mode of healing for Ronny? Do you think she was better off with Ronny than with his brother?

8. *Saving Private Ryan:* When you first watched the Omaha Beach sequence, what was your reaction? Did you feel sad? Queasy? Scared? When you saw that soldier pick up his severed arm, what impression did that give you? How does that alter the respect you have for soldiers fighting in wars?
9. *Finders Keepers:* Why do you think someone like Shannon would want to exploit something as personal to someone as their leg to make money? What does that tell you about the cruel nature of ableism?
10. *In This Corner of the World:* What's your favorite hobby? If you lost the part of your body necessary for accomplishing that task, how would you deal with the trauma? How does Suzu deal with that trauma?
11. Upon watching all these good examples, are there any you believe shouldn't be considered a good example?
12. Now, onto some personal takeaways. Imagine yourself without one or more of your arms or legs, whichever you decide. Now, as you go through your entire day, note all the mundane tasks you do that would require that limb you've selected. How much harder would those tasks be without that limb? What would you do instead? How does that change the way you think of others who need to overcome those obstacles every single day?
13. What new/surprising knowledge did you pick up from reading this chapter?
14. What's the biggest misconception you just learned about limb loss/difference?
15. And most importantly: How will you start to live differently having a new perspective on limb loss/difference?

Chapter 6: Mental Illnesses

My Personal Experience

I remember there being a series on TLC called *My Strange Addiction,* which was all about the bizarre lifestyles some people just couldn't break out of. One woman was addicted to eating toilet paper, another was addicted to eating cat food, and another was addicted to sniffing mothballs. Furthermore, a man was romantically involved with his car, a woman was obsessed over planning out her funeral, and another woman wore fur mascot costumes all the time!

That sort of exposure to strange ways of living is still often found in the things I come across online. Often in the form of shocking headlines or YouTube videos with over a million views, I've learned about these lifestyles real people are living that could very well be categorized as clinical insanity. Some adults have designated time to behave like babies, even going as far as sleeping inside a crib, wearing diapers, drinking baby formula from a bottle, and eating baby food.

While most might call them crazy, the behavior of these people demonstrates a history of abuse in their childhoods, and this infant roleplay is a coping mechanism for them. Frankly, I have that need too, although in my case it's just anything Pokémon or SpongeBob-related, my two childhood special interests that I never officially outgrew. Though if such a coping mechanism went as far as baby roleplay, would it be categorized as a mental illness? I at first thought so, but because these people have reportedly been able to handle other essential issues such as their finances, and their behavior does not interfere with their everyday life, they therefore cannot be categorized as having a disability.

Now, as for real-world exposure, I've had my share of mental illness experiences, in the form of two different roommates who had severe mental health problems. Neither of them was officially diagnosed with anything like clinical depression or anxiety as far as I knew, but they both had overall extremely negative attitudes toward life and liked to rant about their problems toward me whenever they got the chance.

Over their time of living with me, their negativity got from bad to worse—they constantly took advantage of me and would often even accuse me of ruining their lives just for doing things that slightly annoyed them. By now, they're both gone and living their own separate lives, but the trauma of living with each of these mentally unstable people continually haunts me to this day.

As for myself, I've never had any significant disorders aside from my autism, but still had my share of depression, anxiety, and PTSD. Whenever I feel I've done something bad, I get into a period of thinking negative thoughts about myself and am unable to move out of that cycle, often for days. Whenever I felt hopeless about the way my life was going, I was convinced that I no longer had a reason to live.

But since I began to take daily medication, a vast improvement has been made in my overall contentment with life, even though I still had my moments when I got super depressed for several days. Now after becoming a dog owner, my suicidal thoughts are almost nonexistent, and my general mood throughout the year remains positive. She's a sweet little terrier-mix named Bella, and taking care of her and having her love me back unconditionally has given me such immense lasting joy.

Quick Facts

Some types of Mental Illnesses:

- <u>Antisocial Personality Disorder:</u> This overlaps with psychopaths, who often lack a social conscience.
- <u>Anxiety Disorder:</u> The most common type of mental illness, affecting 18.1% of Americans.
- <u>Attention-Deficit/Hyperactivity Disorder (ADHD):</u> Often described as having difficulty in concentrating or fidgeting/performing specific actions without thinking.
- <u>Bipolar Disorder:</u> The person often switches between manic high-energy episodes and depressed low-energy ones. This also can be called "Manic Depression."
- <u>Dissociative Identity Disorder:</u> When someone seems to have more than one distinct identity that their brain switches back and forth between. This was once known as, "Multiple Personality Disorder."
- <u>Eating Disorder:</u> When practice in eating and exercise reaches unhealthy levels of taking over someone's life.
- <u>Narcissistic Personality Disorder:</u> An inflated view of self and inability to empathize with others.
- <u>Obsessive-Compulsive Disorder (OCD):</u> When one has repeated unwanted thoughts or actions, or the urge to do something over and over again.
- <u>Schizophrenia:</u> Only 1% of people have this, it can be developed over time.

Types of schizophrenia:

- <u>Catatonic:</u> A person's movements can be too fast, not fast enough, or unintentionally repetitive.
- <u>Disorganized:</u> This includes disjointed thoughts.

- Paranoid: This includes delusional thoughts.
- Residual: Symptoms still exist, but aren't as intense.
- Undifferentiated: Only a few symptoms from a certain category of schizophrenia are present.

Some causes of a mental illness:

- A mother's exposure to certain substances while pregnant
- Brain injury
- Cancer or infection
- Chemical imbalances in the brain
- Drugs and alcohol
- Exposure to toxic materials
- Hereditary genes passed on from a previous generation
- Loneliness
- Traumatic experiences

Other facts:

- In 2013, it was estimated that about 6.3% of adults in the United States have a mental illness.
- In 2015, 45% of homeless Americans had a mental illness, and 25% had a severe mental illness. Mental illness is also a major cause of someone becoming homeless.
- In 2016, around 20% of jail inmates and 15% of state prison inmates had serious mental illnesses.
- According to research, psychopaths and sociopaths are virtually the same thing.
- People who are psychotic often have schizophrenia.
- Those with mental illnesses are over eleven times more likely to be victims of violent crime.

The Film in Focus

Title	Good Will Hunting
Director	Gus Van Sant
Writer	Ben Affleck, Matt Damon
Main Cast	Matt Damon, Robin Williams
Studio	Miramax
Country	United States
Release	5 December 1997
Runtime	2 hr. 6 min.

Synopsis

Will Hunting is a janitor working for Harvard and secretly solves a linear algebra problem nobody else could solve. He also gets arrested after he and his friends beat up a former bully of his. To avoid jail, the professor who wrote the algebra problem, Mr. Lambeau, proposes he sees a therapist. Lambeau calls in his old friend, Sean, and the first session between Will and Sean turns out to be a near-disaster. However, Sean refuses to give up on Will and continues sessions with him.

Otherwise, Will's future is looking dubious, he won't attend any job interviews, nor join his girlfriend, Skylar, at Stanford. He and Skylar fight over this, and he ultimately leaves her before she gets a chance to abandon him. Sean makes sure to tell Will that he has a horrible tendency of avoiding failure in personal relationships by calling them off. Then Will at last opens up about his traumatic child abuse to Sean, and Sean just tearfully tells him over and over, "it's not your fault." Then sometime later, Will turns down a job offer... but this time so he can head toward California to reunite with Skylar.

The Film's Portrayal of the Disability

The script was originally a school project Matt Damon worked on while he was studying at Harvard, and Ben Affleck, a childhood friend of his, came in to help him finish it. Eventually, it was picked up by Miramax, and they were brought on to also play the starring roles in their script. Once the movie hit theaters, the two were launched into stardom and the movie won the Academy Award for Best Original Screenplay.

It's miraculous to consider how Matt Damon and Ben Affleck, despite not having attachment disorders themselves, were still able to write a masterful script about it. In Matt's case, he could relate a little to Will Hunting, for he did reportedly take medication during the time the movie came out, and admittedly attempted suicide when reviewers never thought to mention his name while talking about the film.

The traits depicted about Will Hunting's attachment disorder aren't explicit, nor do they resort to any stereotypes, for they rely heavily on his fear of abandonment. He only sees every negative thing in every situation and never truly knows anybody on a personal level—because he pushes them all away before they get a chance to leave him. His childhood was a massive contributing factor to how he got this way, not only because he was abused by his father but also because he moved from foster home to foster home a lot. He's not entirely hopeless in this state, however, as Mr. Lambeau recognizes that he has unparalleled photographic intelligence with loads of potential; he's not making the most of his life by being a janitor.

That's why when Will is set up to do jail time, Lambeau instead proposes to help him, offering him therapy so he won't have to go to prison. Yet Will, while insisting that he doesn't need therapy, outsmarts all potential therapists, and thinks he's gotten to Sean by insulting his wife. But Sean doesn't give up that easily, he just asserts himself by telling Will, lovingly, that he's nothing but a cocky scared-shitless kid. Sean then follows that up by saying, "Your move, chief."

By that, Sean means he'll let Will act first—he must want the therapy. Once Will finally does speak in their sessions, the conversations feel much more casual and much less tense, Sean even shares a story about his wife before she died of cancer, and laughs with Will about how she always farted in her sleep loud enough to wake herself up. Without Will noticing it at first, Sean is showing him how the true joy of stuff like marriage comes from the ways we fall short, which Sean intentionally uses to guide Will in his relationships, particularly with Skylar.

So without audiences even noticing it, they are shown by example how healthy constructive therapy is accomplished, the patient should first want to change, and personal connection is essential for someone who has trouble connecting with others.

That reality most comes into play in the climactic scene when Will finally opens up to Sean about his past abuse. Sean had a traumatic history of being abused, so knows exactly how to meet Will where he's at. He just keeps saying to him, "it's not your fault," which is exactly what every victim of trauma needs to hear. Sure enough, this makes Will break at last. I'm no therapist myself, but I believe this movie is just what I need to understand what makes an exceptional doctor.

Though here is the really sad part: Robin Williams was playing that incredible mental health psychologist, however, he couldn't be helped by the same treatment for himself. Robin couldn't find support toward a purpose the same way Will Hunting found his, so on August 11, 2014, Robin Williams died of suicide. This saddening way we lost a celebrity is further evidence that everyone, whether professional psychologists or not, ought to take note of the mastery behind *Good Will Hunting*. It's the rare movie that understands how everybody needs the older generation's guidance to appreciate their own imperfections as well as the imperfections of others.

The Disability in Film History

Unfortunately, many artists need to take better responsibility for the way they've taken advantage of the many existing mental disorders for the sake of entertainment:

The Villain Trope

Many of pop culture's most iconic villains show signs of mental disorders. Sometimes they're simply made to look crazy, such as Alex Forrest in *Fatal Attraction (1987)*, other times they're given split personalities, such as Norman Osborn in *Spider-Man*, Dr. Otto Octavius in *Spider-Man 2*, James McAvoy's character of twenty-four personalities in *Split* and *Glass*, Gollum in *The Lord of the Rings*, or Norman Bates in *Psycho*. Sometimes, the villain gets a specific disorder that tries to be realistic, such as Pseudobulbar Affect (PBA) in *Joker*. In that circumstance, the disability of Batman's infamous foe is used to justify his criminal rebellion, and worse, stereotype people with mental illnesses as being violent terrorists.

The Horror Trope

It's very easy for mental health disorders to translate into modes of fear because several cases indeed prove themselves to be legitimate dangers to others. *Shutter Island* does this by turning its asylum setting into a home for the world's most monstrous criminals who are made even scarier by the constant hiding in shadows, and *Donnie Darko* does this by turning a teen's schizophrenia into a disturbing humanoid rabbit. Each of these cases exploit mental health issues for the sake of foreshadowing and establishing plot twists. *Nightmare Alley (2021)* also briefly features a mentally ill sideshow act being gawked at by carnival patrons as he eats a live chicken, and behind the scenes, the carnival staff beats and cages him with the belief that he truly is part animal.

The Obstacle Trope

In *The Three Faces of Eve,* Eve White has had a split personality named Eve Black since she was six, and the two constantly switch back and forth until a third personality named Jane comes out and kills the two Eves, apparently solving the problem... which obviously would not permanently fix her disorder. *Awakenings (1990)* also plays around with mental illness to challenge the main character by having him cure these patients with catatonia using his breakthrough drug discovery. Each of these examples suggests that mental illnesses can be cured, but for the most part, these types of problems are lifelong.

The Fetish Trope

Lars and the Real Girl features a man who treats his "love doll" as a real person with a full backstory and ethnic background, and his doctor says everyone should support his delusion, as it's considered therapeutic for him. In keeping to that theme of using romance as a cure for mental illness, *Silver Linings Playbook* discards the importance of medication to bring two people together, each with their problems. Then there's *Black Swan,* which does the opposite—various mental disorder symptoms including those from OCD and anxiety are used to generate outrageous imagery, which includes a hot lesbian sex scene that in turn stereotypes homosexuals as being clinically insane and self-destructive.

The Nuisance Trope

The entire plot of *What About Bob?* is centered around a man whose many mental problems include symptoms found in OCD, agoraphobia, and hypochondria. It's a role mostly made for laughs in this comedy film that depicts him as one who gets in the way of his psychiatrist while he and his family are on vacation, which is not okay.

The Inspiration Trope

The Perks of Being a Wallflower depicts a teenage boy with a history of suicide and hospitalizations, and at school, his fellow students call him a "freak" and a "misfit." Rather than show the true tragedy behind his disability, this teen comedy just overlooks it to end on a tearjerker. Also, *A Beautiful Mind* shoves out historical accuracy to inspire the audience with a sentimental story. In real life, John Nash's schizophrenia wasn't quite full of hallucinating visions of specific nonexistent individuals, and he received a medical diagnosis for his condition sometime during his early thirties, not his early twenties.

The Argument that Everyone's a Little Crazy

Unsane is about a woman who is stalked by an older man, but because nobody believes her, she is thrown into a mental hospital. The events from there are meant to ignite questions about whether this victim of sexual harassment has truly just fallen off the deep end, which is ultimately disrespectful to real sexual harassment survivors. Using that same approach, *Girl, Interrupted* tells the true story of Suzanna Kaysen, who upon a Borderline Personality Disorder diagnosis is sent to a ward. She insists that she's not mentally insane, even calling the place a fascist torture chamber, but this movie instead raises the question as to whether she's just driving herself crazy, essentially victim-blaming her.

*****

But gladly, some movies have found the proper balance of portraying such disorders accurately while still being wildly entertaining:

One Flew Over the Cuckoo's Nest (1975) - *United States*

Among the great American films, *One Flew Over the Cuckoo's Nest* flips common misconceptions about the mentally insane by making out the head of the facility, Nurse Ratched, to be a merciless bully over the other men who live there. After Randle tries to pass off as mentally ill to avoid prison and live in the ward instead, his experience under Ratched is far worse than prison could ever be. Yet he still scatters some fruits of labor that give the men a chance to taste the freedom of life, which in turn remedies their issues a little, even beyond Randle's untimely demise.

Amadeus (1984) -*United States*

Salieri's methods of driving Mozart mad even beyond the father's grave prove to be successful. Though many years later, Salieri stumbles down his own path of mental insanity and ultimately ends up in an asylum. While not true to what happened, *Amadeus* is still largely rooted in truth, seeing how in real life, Wolfgang Amadeus Mozart did supposedly have depression, Dependent Personality Disorder, or perhaps even Borderline Personality Disorder.

The Silence of the Lambs (1991) -*United States*

Some in the past have speculated that Hannibal Lecter shows signs of Antisocial Personality Disorder (ASPD), but he doesn't act like a psychopathic prisoner: he's polite, he's patient, he's a gentleman, and most odd of all, he respects Clarice Starling, even if he's just manipulating her to get himself out into the world again. This stands out amongst similar crime thrillers because it proves that those with mental illnesses could be dangerous in ways the media doesn't always show.

Fight Club (1999) -*United States*

Everything the Narrator ever knew about himself falls off the deep end once he meets Tyler, who he starts Fight Club with. Yet the two men are eventually revealed to be the same person—the Narrator's Dissociative Identity Disorder somehow gave him split personalities to the extent he remembers specific events from Tyler's point of view and remembers nothing "Tyler" experienced without him. This wacky satire on late 1990s consumerism gives a different approach to a mental disorder than what would ever be expected.

Little Miss Sunshine (2006) - *United States*

Frank, who has Major Depressive Disorder, got released from the hospital following a suicide attempt, but still lacks any motivation to live. The family road trip he must partake in proves to him an important truth: that they all have their psychological issues, be it the seven-year-old daughter's body image insecurity, the father's struggle to become a financially successful motivational speaker, or the grandfather's porn and drug addiction. Like these things, Major Depressive Disorder is another problem that an everyday family must overcome together; if one member of the family suffers, everyone suffers.

*****

As you go on from here, you'll see mental disorders surfacing everywhere around pop culture, especially in fan theories across the internet. One of those theories has tried to suggest that Winnie-the-Pooh and his friends represent mental illnesses. The prevalence of mental illness discussion across media has been just as prevalent back before the days of the internet as well; before the TV movie *Sybil (1976)* came out, there were only 200 known cases of Multiple Personality Disorder, then after its release, the cases boomed to 8,000 in the United States. So in the future, we can only count on there being a greater presence of mental health disorders in anything we read or watch, especially when new ones are discovered every day.

If you have depression, anxiety, or any other mental health disorder, know that there will always be friends, family members, and professional helpers who love the real you and want to see you become the best version of yourself. And most important of all, remember: It's not your fault.

Discussion Questions

1. What do you think it was about the film in focus, *Good Will Hunting*, that touched so many people? What did its portrayal of mental illnesses have to do with its success?
2. Do you think the relationship between Will and Skylar was a healthy one? If so, how did being with her help him with any form of healing and getting his life together? Or if not, what would have better helped him in his life outside of therapy?
3. Why did Sean saying to Will "it's not your fault" finally give him the healing he needed? Why was it important for Sean to repeat it to him over and over?
4. What does this movie say about what you can do to help a friend or loved one with a mental disorder similar to what Will has?
5. Watch a movie from the "Disability in Film History" section. Do you agree or disagree that the movie is a negative depiction of mental illnesses? Why?
6. *One Flew Over the Cuckoo's Nest:* What did Randle do for the rest of the men in the ward that helped them in their unique problems? What did Nurse Ratched do that worsened their problems?
7. *Amadeus:* How did Mozart's decline into madness hurt his musical career? How was his mental state reflected in the musical compositions he would create? Were they better or worse as a result?
8. *The Silence of the Lambs:* Did you ever feel any sympathy for Hannibal Lecter? Do you think it's appropriate to have that sympathy for serial killers? If not, what are other ways you can think of to humanize any movie antagonist who has a mental illness?

9. *Fight Club:* Did the big plot twist surprise you? What did the plot twist tell you about the true nature of the Narrator? How did it make you question everything in the movie? What does this tell you about people in real life who may have Dissociative Identity Disorder?
10. *Little Miss Sunshine:* Does anyone in your immediate family have mental health problems similar to the family in this movie? Looking at your own experience, how has the family members' mental health disorders brought everyone closer together? How has it drifted them apart?
11. Upon watching all these good examples, are there any you believe shouldn't be considered a good example?
12. Now, onto some personal takeaways. Next time you watch a movie you're very familiar with, try to imagine what those same events of the entire movie would be like from the point-of-view of the villain. For example, if it were *The Wizard of Oz (1939)*, try to think of what the movie would be like if the Wicked Witch of the West was the main character, and the antagonist was Dorothy. How does this thinking change the way you think of people who are often depicted as the bad guy? How would this change the way you think of people in the real world with mental health issues?
13. What new/surprising knowledge did you pick up from reading this chapter?
14. What's the biggest misconception you just learned about mental illnesses?
15. And most importantly: How will you start to live differently having a new perspective on mental illnesses?

Chapter 7: Memory Loss

My Personal Experience

I once had a great-aunt named Rachel who lived in Sierra Vista, Arizona. Throughout my childhood, my family loved seeing her whenever we visited my grandparents, who also lived in Sierra Vista. Auntie Rachel, my grandpa's sister, really brought a big spark of joy into every room she was in, and while not around her, my family had such fun imitating the silly things she would say, such as, "Now, now, now, Trayvor (that's how she pronounced my name), you are just... so... GOOD at drawing! My WORD! Goodness, GRACIOUS!"

By the time I hit high school, she needed to move into an assisted-living facility and was openly deteriorating. She always needed to walk with someone by her side, and her attention span was noticeably slower. Those things just came with her aging, but after a few more years, she was diagnosed with Dementia.

I only saw her once when she had Dementia, and only for about an hour, but it was not a pretty sight. She no longer recognized anyone in the family, we all had to remind her who we were and how we were related to her. She didn't even recognize a photo on the wall of her younger self. She no longer looked like herself, and just felt like a shell of a person. Two years after that day, on October 16, 2012, my Auntie Rachel passed away. Although we were all sad, the timing worked out, because by then, she had officially lost her quality of life.

That was my only exposure to a real-life person with Alzheimer's or Dementia. Any previous exposure wasn't enough to make me see just how frightening and heartbreaking the disease is.

I watched an awful lot of TV as a kid, which meant I naturally saw many common patterns in episode plot lines. One of those would involve a character acquiring temporary amnesia after a sharp bonk on the head, or maybe even believing that they were someone else entirely, such as the King of France. Nearly every time in these episodes, the person's memory would come back once they were hit on the head again. I realize it was never meant to be realistic, but back then, I did believe that memory loss and restoration did indeed work that way.

On that note, think of the kids watching their favorite cartoons who would start throwing rocks at their friends to remove their memories or make them think they were a whole new person. You could see the danger there, especially since I know from experience that kids embrace the art of imitation.

I only recall one time on TV when I watched an episode that depicted memory loss realistically and respectfully. It was the *Full House* episode, *The Volunteer (1991)* when DJ volunteered to spend time with a man at a retirement home, whom she later found out has Alzheimer's. The episode hit me hard because the man's memory loss was never played for laughs, but was shown for the serious, tragic prison that it is.

Nowadays, I'm noticing more how people over the age of sixty-five show signs of many disabilities, with memory loss being one of them. I've seen some of those older folk, such as my grandparents, forget certain details such as what they ate for breakfast that morning, and would even mix up people's names. It's gotten me thinking about the ways media has historically misrepresented the elderly, which often goes hand-in-hand with misrepresenting disability.

Quick Facts

Types of Dementia:

- Frontotemporal: When nerve cells in the frontal and temporal lobes of the brain break down.
- Lewy Body: When protein clumps form around the brain. This can lead to symptoms similar to Parkinson's disease.
- Vascular: When damage is caused to the blood vessels that lead to the brain.
- Alzheimer's: When plaques and tangles are developed in the brain, damaging the neurons and fibers.

Types of Alzheimer's:

- Sporadic: (90-95% of cases) A late onset, often genetic.
- Familial: (5-10% of cases) An early onset, often a dominant gene.

Some causes of Dementia:

- Down Syndrome
- Hearing Loss
- Parkinson's Disease
- Traumatic Brain Injury

Other facts:

- 40% of people living with Dementia have depression.
- Dementia is more common in people over the age of sixty-five.
- For many families who have a person with Dementia in their household, the cost of their care can take up at least 32% of their total annual income.

The Film in Focus

Title	Memento
Director	Christopher Nolan
Writer	Christopher Nolan, Jonathan Nolan
Main Cast	Guy Pearce, Joe Pantoliano
Studio	Newmarket Capital Group
Country	United States
Release	25 May 2001
Runtime	1 hr. 53 min.

Synopsis

Leonard Shelby has anterograde amnesia and needs aids to help him sustain recent memories, be it Polaroid photographs or self-applied tattoos. He believes he found his wife's rapist and murderer, but the points which brought him there may not be reliable. Therefore, the film's chronology starts playing backward from there; he tells himself in a Polaroid photo that the man he just killed, Teddy, is untrustworthy, and as his memories continually come up, the dependability of everybody he comes across, including himself, is questioned.

By the end of this trip back in time, Leonard believes he found the perpetrator, using Teddy's help, with whom Leonard immediately strangles and swaps clothes. Yet Teddy gives Leonard some more information that dispels the belief that this man was the rapist and murderer of his wife. Teddy goes on to say that he found and killed the real rapist a year earlier, which Leonard wouldn't know anyway. Leonard lies to himself by writing a false reminder to himself that Teddy is the guy he's seeking to kill.

The Film's Portrayal of the Disability

The main message of this movie is, "facts, not memories, that's how you investigate." That idea may ring true sometimes, but *Memento* doesn't stick to that idea strongly enough. While its portrayal of Anterograde Memory Loss is accurate, the issue of its portrayal of memory loss disorders more so lies in what role it plays in the story... an obstacle for getting plot information across, like many disabilities used in storytelling.

Right from the start, Christopher Nolan's groundbreaking script was conceptualized as a compelling thriller that goes against traditional writing. Christopher Nolan was inspired by a short story written by his brother and altered that concept into a feature-length suspense thriller designed to benefit from repeated viewings. He never even thought of it as being linear. He started writing from the very first scene (chronologically the last) and the final scene he wrote was the last one (chronologically the first). He wrote it with inspiration from the film noir genre because he's drawn to the concept that nobody can ever count on anybody, not even themselves.

In directing the film, he broke it up between two separate timelines that go back and forth throughout the film. The scenes in color take place from Leonard's point of view and go backward in time, while the black-and-white scenes are written from an objective point of view and go forward in time. Ultimately, the two timelines meet at the end.

There are instances of hidden details that prove how clever the imagination Christopher Nolan is, which are all subtle enough to only be noticed by the careful watcher, yet open to interpretation enough to speak differently to different types of viewers.

The way Leonard writes on his hand to remember things is a play on the phrase, "know it like the back of my hand," and the reminder he tapes onto his leg, which says "shave," could mean several things, not just shaving his leg hair. Maybe he must remove the hair of (or emasculate) a certain man? Maybe he needs to shave somebody else's, ahem, NECK? Leonard treats the rest of his body as a canvas for reminders, which he tattoos all over his body with a regular everyday pen as if he's identifying himself as a victim of revenge.

However, given the overall big picture the details are a part of, there's very little miraculous content that makes this distinct from other movies of this genre. Christopher Nolan didn't do enough to build a multidimensional romance between Leonard and Natalie, as well as a strong enough friendship/rivalry between Leonard and Teddy. Natalie is at the end of the day nothing more than a drop-dead gorgeous femme fatale who thinks Leonard is weak because of his condition. She even calls him a "retard" and a "freak" right to his face, knowing he would forget she ever did it a minute later.

That's just one instance of how nearly every character takes advantage of Leonard's memory loss and gets in his way. A particular subplot further hammers in the point that memory loss is something for nondisabled people to exploit selfishly.

A man named Sammy has a condition similar to Leonard's. A doctor gives him a test in which he chooses from a set of geometric shapes on his desk to pick up, one of which would shock him if he touched it. The purpose of the experiment is to see if his condition is in the situation of memory being connected to instinct rather than memory. Sure enough, he fails the test constantly, proving that his condition is psychological instead of physical.

This very much hurts Sammy's wife, who claims she misses the old Sammy. Although this isn't nearly as hurtful for the audience because they never get to know what the old Sammy was like, there's no comparison point to understand the tragedy. On that note, his wife has a test of her own. She repeatedly lies to him and sets her watch back to the time she needs a shot of insulin, getting way too many injections than what's safe in under an hour. This ends up being her method of committing suicide, and no sense of reconciliation is given to Sammy. He's just a forever victim of his memory loss.

More of the terrible messages in this movie demean the reality behind memory loss disorders, turning them into weapons that one can play to their benefit. Leonard feeds himself constant lies, knowing that moments later he'll forget the truth and believe the lie he told himself was true. In the end, he becomes neither a likable character nor a character who goes through any change, but someone who only remembers whatever he wishes were true, which is a very dangerous attitude for anyone to practice, whether they're disabled or not.

Nobody should exploit people that way for a movie designed to treat the disability community as the "mysterious other." Likewise, nondisabled audiences ought to be more cautious of movies that try to make out people with memory loss as complex codes to crack.

The Disability in Film History

The act of removing and/or replacing memories has become a frequent tool writers use to make plot progression easier or make specific plot points more shocking. It's become so common that this casual treatment of the disorder has lessened the sympathy toward those who lose their memories in real life for several reasons.

The Horror Trope

In *Moon,* Sam acquires brain damage while he's alone on the moon, and remembers nothing besides the name of his robot companion. Then right after his accident, he's met by a clone of himself, and the film leaves it up to interpretation as to whether this clone is real or just a hallucination that came about due to his memory loss. Similarly, Jason Bourne from the *Bourne* series has no recollection of his past and somehow possesses all these special combat skills. The long quest to rediscover his background is designed to raise stakes. Though the most direct association of a specific memory loss disorder to horror happens in *Hereditary* when Annie mentions how her mother had Dementia, foreshadowing how her disabled mother later becomes one of the film's core villains.

The "Other" Trope

It's a common idea throughout sci-fi: various characters having brains that function more like a computer's memory drive which can be rebooted and reconfigured with a new set of information. This has been done in *Blade Runner, Blade Runner 2049, RoboCop, Total Recall, Ghost in the Shell (1995), Men in Black II,* and *Alita: Battle Angel.* Furthermore, the droids from the *Star Wars* series are all capable of having their memories erased by their masters; when one stops to think about it, taking away the memories of sentient souls, even if they're just robots, is pretty sadistic. Also in *Pokémon Detective Pikachu,* that little talking electric mouse who teams up with the hero is later revealed to be a human whose soul was put in the creature's body without any memory of his life as a human. These instances of treating memories like flexible digital data create a false notion that memory loss disorders aren't all that bad.

The Obstacle Trope

Welcome to Marwen retells the true story of Mark Hogancamp and his miniature WWII doll village built to reclaim his lost memories after a combat assault, which just treats his memory disorder like a roadblock to overcome. Yet this type of trope has been more prevalent in *Still Alice*, which features a woman who gets Alzheimer's at quite an early age and goes through the symptoms quickly, a tragic condition she never truly learns to accept. Furthermore, *Coco (2017)* features memory loss in Mamá Coco as her memories slowly fade away, making her deceased father risk being forgotten entirely from the land of the dead, and thus fading away from existence forever. It's meant to give Miguel a ticking timebomb back in the land of the living to restore Mamá Coco's memory of her father.

The Magical/Supernatural Trope

Memory erasure has often been treated like it's a force only found within magical worlds. Such examples include *Hook (1991), Spirited Away, Your Name., Beauty and the Beast (2017), Spider-Man: No Way Home,* the "obliviate" charm from the *Harry Potter* movies, Anna having her memories of Elsa's ice powers erased in *Frozen,* and the Pensive children over time losing all memories of their previous lives back home in *The Chronicles of Narnia: The Lion, the Witch, and the Wardrobe.*

The Pity Trope

In *On Golden Pond,* Norman just turned eighty and has shown many signs of Alzheimer's, including sudden inappropriate outbursts when not warranted. His story arc tries hard to be an emotional, weepy character study about a man denying his fear of death, yet it actually traps him in this condition that's written for excessive drama so audiences could cry over the fact that he must spend the last of his days in gradual memory decay.

The Comic Relief Trope

Dory from *Finding Nemo* and *Finding Dory* remains a widely beloved character across many generations, although there is danger in how her short-term memory loss is her defining character trait. Nearly every time Dory's memory loss is brought up, it's played for laughs. The whole *Men in Black* series also uses the memory eraser devices mostly for laughs. The first installment has Agents Kay and Jay visiting a woman's house after her husband had just become alien food; after getting the needed information, Kay erases her memories and verbally feeds her a new memory to replace them, which Jay decides to have some fun with. He tells her she kicked her husband out of the house and that she should now seize the moment to stitch her life back together with a personal makeover, including a facial.

The Plot Device Trope

In *Spider-Man 3,* the writers decided to erase Harry Osborn's memory for a while because too many plot threads were going on simultaneously and they needed a way to shove him aside until he was needed again. In *Captain America: The Winter Soldier,* Bucky can't remember Steve, so he becomes an antagonistic force that drives the movie. In *The Memory of a*

Killer, a mob hitman with Alzheimer's struggles to remember things that are crucial for revealing important plot information. These are only a few instances of memory loss being used to make getting toward a certain mode of conflict easier.

The Victim Trope

Away From Her presents a bleak survey of Dementia from the perspective of Fiona's husband, who must watch her slowly disappear and fail to remember that he's even her husband. In the end, he must come to accept that the old Fiona he once knew shall remain a mere memory forever, leaving their fate together on a hopeless note. On a similar note, the final act of *The Curious Case of Benjamin Button* features Benjamin acquiring Alzheimer's disease when he reaches his old *ahem* YOUNG age (since he ages backward). He no longer recognizes Daisy, the woman he loved for most of his life, and she must watch over him until he dies as a baby.

*****

Movies that truthfully depict memory loss are very few, but some miraculously do demonstrate a keen understanding of why losing memories can become so tragic:

Eternal Sunshine of the Spotless Mind (2004) -*United States*

Joel and Clementine broke up, and Clementine underwent a scientific procedure to erase every memory of him. Joel takes on the same procedure, except later he goes back and sees the happy memories he and Clementine shared, which makes him realize that he would rather not lose her. This ambitious art-house piece breaks all the rules of screenwriting to give a deep psychological dive into romance and breakups, showing why certain people just can't afford to be forgotten, even amidst the tough times.

A Separation (2011) -*Iran*

Nader's wife intends to leave town, and even divorce him if he refuses to join her, however, he must stay at home to care for his father, who has Alzheimer's. Nader hires a pregnant caretaker, Razieh, who one day locks the door on the old man and ties his hand to the bedpost before she leaves for a doctor's visit. When Nader arrives home, Razieh is still gone, and his father fell onto the floor, almost dead. This starts an ugly chain of events that causes Razieh's miscarriage, assumedly because of Nader angrily pushing her down the stairs. The ultimate testament of this high-stakes domestic drama is how much Alzheimer's challenges the commitment between family members.

First Cousin Once Removed (2012) -*United States*

Edwin no longer recognizes Alan, his first cousin once removed, no matter how many times they meet across the years. In the series of meetings portrayed in this documentary, Alan records the seventy-year-old man going through his old photographs, home videos, letters, and works of poetry, hardly any of which are successful at bringing the memories back. *First Cousin Once Removed* offers a complete and cohesive analysis of Alzheimer's, and affirms that whatever happens to Edwin, he will never lose his life's true purpose of being a poet.

Logan (2017) -*United States*

Professor Charles Xavier is no longer the powerful figure from previous *X-Men* movies, now, he has a degenerative brain disease. As he makes his way toward the grave, Xavier reflects on the life he once enjoyed, which he sees represented often in nostalgic Hollywood westerns. While director James Mangold could have easily made this conclusion to Wolverine and Professor X's stories yet another overblown messy superhero flick, he instead wisely made it a character study grounded in reality.

The Father (2021) - *United Kingdom*

Anthony Hopkins plays a man with Dementia whose memories are no longer arranged in a linear pattern. One minute, his single daughter lives with him in his flat, the next minute, she's much younger and married, and the next, he's confined to a hospital bed. The final scene shows him in a pitiful hopeless state, where he has nothing left to say other than, "I want my mommy." This frightening depiction of Dementia is not only heartbreaking to watch, but it can help many more families who are caring for a victim of this unforgiving disease.

*****

The studying I've done for this chapter has certainly made me consider more just how much movies and TV shows like to bash the elderly, who naturally develop disabilities, whether it's sudden mood swings, loss of sight, loss of hearing, loss of speech, inability to walk, or incapacity to remember things. Hopefully, reading this chapter will ignite related topics of discussion for you too.

Discussion Questions

1. The film in focus, *Memento,* is still considered a highly ambitious screenplay. Do you agree that the script is as brave or as clever as people claim it is?
2. Is there ever a proper comeuppance given to the characters who take advantage of Leonard's condition? If not, how would you change the story so that they get what they deserve?
3. Do you think this movie has anything to say about how to help one with a memory loss disorder? Or about how one with a memory loss disorder can help themselves?
4. Would you call Leonard a hero or an antihero? If he's a hero, does his condition help or hinder his goal? If he's an antihero, do you believe that he's there to depict people with disabilities as criminals?
5. Watch a movie from the "Disability in Film History" section. Do you agree or disagree that the movie is a negative depiction of memory loss? Why?
6. *Eternal Sunshine of the Spotless Mind:* Is there a specific person in your life you wish you could erase all memory of? What would happen to you if your wish was granted? Do you think you'd be happier?
7. *A Separation:* Do you think that Razieh was in the right for leaving Nader's father locked in his room while she went to the doctor? If not, what do you think was a better course of action she could have taken?
8. *First Cousin Once Removed:* What would you say the concept of memory means to you? Are they similar to the tree and leaf metaphor Alan presents here? What other illustration would you use?

9. *Logan:* If you've seen the other *X-Men* movies, how does this unfamiliar version of Professor X make you feel? Are you disappointed or saddened? What does his brain disease have to say about how superheroes have shaped America's definition of heroism?
10. *The Father:* Is Anthony's nonlinear way of recalling events what you often think of when you think about Dementia? What about this depiction of Dementia was unexpected for you? Based on this movie, what's the best way to care for a relative who has a memory disorder this severe?
11. Upon watching all these good examples, are there any you believe shouldn't be considered a good example?
12. Now, onto some personal takeaways. Imagine what it would be like for you if one day your father or mother no longer recognized who you were. What if they couldn't recall the countless years' worth of memories with you? What if they thought you were a stranger in their home and wanted you out? Or what if you went down that cycle yourself? What if you could no longer recognize your children, spouse, or old photographs of yourself? What if you forgot you ever even had a spouse or kids? How scary do you think that would be? What do you think your day-to-day existence would be like?
13. What new/surprising knowledge did you pick up from reading this chapter?
14. What's the biggest misconception you just learned about memory loss?
15. And most importantly: How will you start to live differently having a new perspective on memory loss?

ём # Chapter 8: Motor Impairment

My Personal Experience

I remember the Ice Bucket Challenge in the summer of 2014, which also was the first time I heard about ALS (or Lou Gehrig's Disease). The challenge started as a way to raise awareness about ALS. Someone on Facebook would post a video pouring a bucket of ice water onto themselves, then nominate three other people to do the same. But nobody ever nominated me for the challenge, which confirmed my fear that I was nobody's three closest friends, and ultimately the ALS Ice Bucket Challenge left me with nothing but negative emotions.

Yet looking back on it now, I'm a bit glad I wasn't nominated to do the challenge because I currently believe the challenge was morally wrong. While it did help raise awareness and profits for the disease, the whole thing became a dumb internet fad for the sake of entertainment. Everyone forgot the entire reason the challenge originally began.

During that time, I noticed how my sister responded when she was nominated for the challenge. She didn't pour ice water on herself, she didn't post a video, she instead made a Facebook post saying that she gave a donation to an ALS charity, and said to her followers, "you're all nominated!" I admire how my sister understood the big cause and kept to her beliefs.

And funnily enough, the same year the Ice Bucket Challenge came and went, *The Theory of Everything* was released, which showed Stephen Hawking's battle against Lou Gehrig's Disease. So of course, Eddie Redmayne won the Oscar for playing this role while the internet fad was still fresh in everyone's memory. Then a few years after the challenge, Stephen Hillenburg, the creator of *SpongeBob SquarePants,* died of ALS. Next to Robin Williams, this celebrity death devastated me the most, because he created my childhood hero.

Besides that one viral challenge, I've had other relevant exposures to different motor impairment disorders. A roommate of mine had multiple sclerosis, which meant a lot of the time she had difficulty standing, and simple tasks like tearing apart pieces of paper caused her too much pain. On some days, she walked around okay, but on other days, she needed canes and crutches, and on other days still, she could not stand by herself at all. Before I met her, I didn't even have any idea that multiple sclerosis existed.

I've seen some temporary foot impairment happen in my family before, such as my Mom getting surgery on her foot and afterward needing assistance from me and my Dad. Plus, my sister played soccer throughout her grade school and middle school years, and hurt her ankle during one of her matches. Over the next couple of weeks, her ankle grew bluish-purple and horribly swollen, perhaps double its usual size! As for myself, I never needed a wheelchair or crutches at any point in my life, heck, I've never even broken a bone. Although there were times when I hurt my ankle and had to wear a bandage wrap, and other times when I simply felt unexplained knee/ankle pain and had to walk around on a limp.

Those few examples within my family were far from permanent disabilities, but prove how nobody needs one to get an idea of what it's like to be motor-impaired. It goes to show how a disability really can happen to anyone on any day for any length of time.

Quick Facts

Some types of motor impairment:

- <u>Arthritis:</u> The inflammation of one or more joints, which worsens with age.
- <u>Cerebral Palsy:</u> The most common motor impairment for children, this hinders the ability to move and sustain balance.
- <u>Essential Tremor:</u> This causes rhythmic shaking, mostly in the hands.
- <u>Lou Gehrig's Disease:</u> Also called Amyotrophic Lateral Sclerosis (ALS), this causes the degrading of muscles needed for speech, digestion, breathing, and mobility.
- <u>Multiple Sclerosis:</u> This causes communication problems between the brain and the rest of the body.
- <u>Muscular Dystrophy:</u> This involves progressive weakness and loss of muscle mass.
- <u>Parkinson's Disease:</u> A brain disorder that causes uncontrollable muscle movement.
- <u>Spina Bifida:</u> At birth, an improperly formed spinal column leaves a bit of the spinal cord and nerves exposed in the back.

Some potential causes of motor impairment:

- Brain Injury
- Cardiac Disease
- Limb Loss/Difference
- Musculoskeletal Injury
- Obesity
- Old Age
- Respiratory Disease
- Stroke

Some aids to help people with motor impairment:

- Adaptive Keyboard
- Automatic Page Turner
- Cane
- Crutches
- Eye Tracking Software
- Head Wand
- Mouth Stick
- Oversized Trackball Mouse
- Scooter
- Screen Reader
- Single-Switch Access
- Sip and Puff Switch
- Voice Recognition Software
- Walker
- Wheelchair

Other essential facts:

- 40% of people with motor impairment have difficulty using their hands.
- As of 2013, it was estimated that 41.8% of people with paralysis were unable to work.
- As of 2015, there were approximately 2.7 million full-time wheelchair users in the United States, by 2019, the number reached 3 million.
- Stroke is the leading cause of paralysis, with the second being spinal cord injury.
- It's reported that wheelchair-accessible taxis are in very short supply across the United States, especially in small towns.

The Film in Focus

Title	The Diving Bell and the Butterfly
Director	Julian Schnabel
Writer	Ronald Harwood
Main Cast	Mathieu Amalric, Marie-Josée Croze
Studio	Pathé
Country	France
Release	23 May 2007
Runtime	1 hr. 52 min.

Synopsis

Jean-Dominique Bauby (or Jean-Do) wakes up in a hospital, now paralyzed from head to toe with cerebrovascular action, AKA "Locked-In Syndrome." His left eye is the only part of his body he can still move. He meets his two physiotherapists, and their divine beauty helps him recollect his memories from right before his fateful stroke. One of these ladies develops a communication system: by verbalizing every letter in the alphabet, and him blinking at the letter he wants her to stop on; they repeat the process until the letters he blinks to make a word.

He is visited by Céline, the mother of his children, but his thoughts rather linger on another woman named Inès, and on his old and frail father. His predicament still doesn't look good over time, but Jean-Do decides to write a book about his state, which takes him 200,000 blinks to complete and is also the very book this movie was adapted from. He describes the feeling as being in a diving bell (or an old metal suit worn by scuba divers) while everyone else sees him as a lively and delicate butterfly. Then ten days after the book hits store shelves, he dies.

The Film's Portrayal of the Disability

The Diving Bell and the Butterfly has gained worldwide acclaim with its top-notch directing and inspiring real-life story, although the biography about Jean-Dominique Bauby still embraces the same inspirational tropes seen in the negative examples throughout this book, mostly of him becoming an object of pity who does the impossible, thus encouraging nondisabled audiences to do better with themselves.

Like any biopic, the credibility of this movie's message depends heavily on its accuracy to the real events. Unfortunately, there are many details the script intentionally skews for dramatic effect. First of all, the mother of his kids wasn't named Céline, but Sylvie de la Rouchefoucauld, and Inès' real name was Florence Ben Sadoun. Sylvie also showed Jean-Do greater faithfulness at the hospital than the film depicts, and Florence didn't refuse to see Jean-Do out of fear from seeing him in his present state, she saw him far more frequently than Sylvie did.

As extra bonuses to the altering of truth, the real Jean-Do had two children rather than three, and he never said he wanted to die. I understand how changing names could be a logical change, to protect the privacy of some of the real-life people, but giving him one extra child? And changing the people's personalities? And changing his desires? That's completely insulting.

But what about his condition? How is that portrayed? Well, from the research I found, it checks out well. Right from when he wakes up after a near-three-week coma, his memories start vague, and gradually come back to him over time. Shortly after he awakens from the coma, his right eye is occluded by the hospital staff to protect his cornea from going septic. Right away, the audience feels almost as terrified as the real Jean-Do must have felt, which becomes all the more effective by the first-person point-of-view the film's first third takes on.

Other details show how his predicament, while not ideal, still could find methods of doing things differently. He can't embrace his kids anymore, but he can still play certain games with them such as hangman. The men who set up his speaker phone make rude remarks right to his face, but secretly, he thinks their jokes were funny. He may not be able to bathe himself anymore, but he can still be given one by the doctors (which is humiliating). And most importantly, while he may not be able to speak or move anymore, he can still communicate through the complex system his physiotherapists developed.

But there's another important thing he hasn't lost—his imagination. While he sees his existence as a beach on an island where he can't go to explore any beautiful sights, he can still do so in his mind. He exercises his freedom to imagine without limits and play God inside his place without any interfering religion. He's not like the other religious folk around the world who pray in ways that he sees as cultish. He can make up his own religion, one that degrades the attractive women in his life into nothing more than tools.

Not a single female character in this movie has any character development—even a fly that lands on Jean-Do's nose has more personality than any of them. The reason for that is because this film is told from the perspective of the director and writers, who assume the male gaze in every scene and every frame. Despite this being a PG-13 movie, there's an uncomfortable amount of female nudity in sexual contexts, and Jean-Do has a fantasy where he steps out of his wheelchair and kisses an attractive woman. It's the old Hollywood cliché of women only existing to fulfill male fetishes and motivate them to keep pushing forward, ultimately degrading their personalities to being whatever men want them to be.

What does that sexism have to do with disability representation though? It's because those stereotypes differ between men and women: disabled men can become heroes, but disabled women are broken. That appears elsewhere in examples throughout this book, especially in *City Lights* and *Freaks*.

There are more ways *The Diving Bell and the Butterfly* disgraces the idea of motor impairment. It's reported near the end that he could sing and talk a tiny bit, but he's never seen actually doing it. But the most insulting part is when Jean-Do is on the phone with his father, who tells his son that he believes he too lives with a locked-in condition just because he's so old. While this conversation overall is emotionally very powerful, limitations due to old age are nowhere near the same thing as Locked-In Syndrome. Nobody should ever believe that toxic idea.

Despite how well the production expertly tricks the average moviegoer into thinking it's an intelligent, profound, artistic masterpiece, nobody should be smooth-talked into how pretty it looks on the surface. Deep down, women deserve better, anyone who has motor impairment deserves better, and most importantly, humanity deserves better. This all can be summed up by a quote from Brice Agnelli, a friend of the real Florence Ben Sadoun: "It's not the story of my friend, it's a story for Hollywood."

The Disability in Film History

Somewhere between twenty and thirty real paraplegics helped film *Saving Private Ryan's* Omaha Beach sequence, and Lionel Barrymore (Mr. Potter from *It's a Wonderful Life)* was a wheelchair user in real life. Those are a few rare times a movie features actual people with motor impairment, but otherwise, they're underrepresented in film.

The Inspiration Trope

The true stories of Christy Brown in *My Left Foot,* Ron Kovic in *Born on the Fourth of July,* Stephen Hawking in *The Theory of Everything,* and Stuart Long in *Father Stu* have shown men overcoming their conditions to change the world. Likewise, there's a scene in *Pearl Harbor* where President Franklin D. Roosevelt says he believes God took away his ability to walk so that he can stand up alongside America and fight together. These examples mean well, but use their stories only as motivation for nondisabled viewers.

The Dominance Trope

In *Willy Wonka and the Chocolate Factory,* Charlie's four grandparents have stayed in a large bed together for twenty years straight, that is, until Grandpa Joe sees that Charlie won a golden ticket. Then suddenly, a miracle! He can walk again! But that isn't the only time this movie makes a jab at walking impairment. When Gene Wilder was offered the role of the famous chocolatier, he said he would only accept the role if he were allowed to make his entrance while limping. These two details create an image that anybody with those types of disabilities can't compare to fame and fortune.

The Pity Trope

Everybody knows that the super-cute child with cerebral palsy, Tiny Tim, acts practically saint-like in every *A Christmas Carol* adaptation, and it's enough to make his death all the sadder. Yet this trope happens more in war movies; *The Men (1950)* and *Coming Home* both show soldiers returning from war in a wheelchair, and neither one finds their sense of purpose again until they've been accepted by a woman.

The Comic Relief Trope

In *Mary and Max,* Max has a pet snail named after Stephen Hawking, and it appropriately looks all askew in its contorted body. In *Mean Girls,* a girl in a wheelchair falls backward into the crowd of junior girls at the assembly scene, and later, Regina George wears a ridiculous neck brace after her school bus injury. A few more examples of using the condition for comic relief are in *Dr. Strangelove, The Big Lebowski,* and the whole "blind beggar" scene in *Trading Places (1983).*

The Worthlessness Trope

As stated in the Limb Loss/Difference chapter, the finale of *Million Dollar Baby* gives the horrible message that euthanizing a permanently disfigured victim is the merciful thing to do, because their life at that point is worthless. But this same toxic mindset is present in *Me Before You,* which says that someone in a wheelchair for life can only find freedom by suicide.

The Victimization Trope

In *What Ever Happened to Baby Jane?,* a psychopathic woman torments her paraplegic sister. In *The Texas Chain Saw Massacre,* a teenage boy in a wheelchair is among the several victims of

Leatherface. In *Awakenings (1990),* the catatonic patients are seen as pitiful in comparison to the doctor who cures them. In *Gattaca,* a wheelchair user is put in to show what an imperfect human looks like. In *Kill Bill Vol. 1,* the bride at the start of her quest for revenge loses mobility in her legs and must spend hours lying down, saying to herself, "wiggle your big toe." In *Shutter Island,* Teddy's palsy is used to further sell the concept of his mental instability, which foreshadows the big reveal about himself toward the end.

The Superhuman Trope

Both *Avatar* and *Upgrade (2018)* create fantasies where someone with limited mobility gets a chance to move around in a super advanced body, and Professor Charles Xavier in the X-Men franchise compensates for his mobility limitation with his amazing brainpower. Plus, the *Harry Potter* series uses the curse, "Petrificus Totalus," which causes a target's entire body to freeze like stone. All of these scenarios turn disabilities into a tool that creates fantastical weapons.

The Villain Trope

This includes Mr. Potter, Mr. Glass from *Unbreakable* and *Glass,* the "Big" Lebowski, and Howard Cliff from *Pokémon Detective Pikachu.* Plus, many sources have stated how behind the scenes of *Morbius,* Jared Leto moved around on a wheelchair or crutches as a way of getting in character, being the method actor that he is. But of course, the movie ended up getting dreadful reviews, proving his attempt at a powerful performance to be a failure, and proving how his acting methods in that scenario were in extremely poor taste.

*****

Considering how common motor impairment is in the many decades of film history, some movies have done it right:

Midnight Cowboy (1969) - *United States*

Enrico "Ratso" Rizzo, a con man who limps, has no way to survive in New York other than by hustling the rich. He hopes moving to Miami could provide him a taste of freedom, except because of his deteriorating health, he may not meet his goal. Sure enough, when his new friend Joe puts him on a Miami-bound bus, he grows sicker until he passes away. The result of this depressing movie is a voice given to a poor man whose demise could have been prevented had the societal system not failed him.

Breaking the Waves (1996) -*Denmark*

After a terrible accident on the oil rig, Bess's husband Jan is now bound to a respirator and may never walk again. Bess wonders if God is testing her commitment to her husband, and that very well does seem to be the case. Jan makes Bess have sex with other men so she could describe to him what it feels like since he has forgotten what love feels like. Her fulfillment of Jan's desire ultimately brings the two of them sheer devastation rather than fulfillment, which leaves them in permanent disarray.

Downfall (2004) -*Germany*

In Adolf Hitler's last few days before his eventual suicide, his rattling hand secretly provides evidence of Parkinson's disease, which coupled with the war's end amplifies his sheer downfall after a powerful career. Few artists would be brave enough to show the humanity behind who history calls one of the evilest men ever, yet the inclusion of Parkinson's disease is a reminder of how this "fascist monster" was more vulnerable than assumed.

The Favourite (2018) -*United Kingdom*

Behind the scenes of the castle, Queen Anne's gout (a form of arthritis) makes her a vulnerable target for her two closest female companions, Sarah and Abigail, as they each ignite a civil war to exploit her weak state through lesbian affairs. It's made clear how the war happening outside between England and France was intensified because some women inside saw their ruler's pitiful state in a wheelchair as a source of exploitation.

Crip Camp (2020) -*United States*

Executive produced by Barack and Michelle Obama, *Crip Camp* stands out for how it enables their community to finally speak up for themselves. There is a brimming "separate but equal" hierarchy among them based on whoever looks the most nondisabled, yet they still unite for a common cause. Fifty paraplegics blocked a Manhattan traffic intersection during a 1972 protest, and the Capitol Crawl of 1990 led to the groundbreaking Americans with Disabilities Act of 1990.

*****

Along with all these different stories to tell about motor impairment, filmmakers haven't even scratched the surface of the potential. For instance, there's never been a movie about facial paralysis (aka Bell's Palsy), which a few celebrities have, including Angelina Jolie, George Clooney, and Sylvester Stallone. More movies focused on paralysis need to be made, so we can work and hope for an ideal future of stronger representation.

Discussion Questions

1. The film in focus, *The Diving Bell and the Butterfly,* has been widely acclaimed around the world. Aside from its inspiring depiction of motor impairment, what do you think led to its praise as a masterpiece?
2. How do you think the film would play differently if the characters were all 100% accurate to their real-life counterparts? Would the story be better or worse?
3. How would you rewrite the story so that all the female characters had an arc, ergo, were different in the end compared to the beginning? How would that change its portrayal of Locked-In Syndrome?
4. If the real Jean-Dominique Bauby was alive today and saw this movie, do you think that he would like it? Why or why not?
5. Watch a movie from the "Disability in Film History" section. Do you agree or disagree that the movie is a negative depiction of motor impairment? Why?
6. *Midnight Cowboy:* What did you think of Ratso as a character? Do you think he's likable or unlikable? Does the fact that he had a limp or an illness have anything to do with his likability? How would you rewrite his character to make him easier to sympathize with?
7. *Breaking the Waves:* How do you think Bess's faith was being put to the test when Jan was injured and bedridden? Do you think she failed that test? Similarly, how do you think Jan was being tested in his horrible condition? Did he pass or fail his test?
8. *Downfall:* When you saw Hitler's hand shaking from behind his back, did that give you any sign of sympathy toward this dictator? Do you feel bad for feeling sorry for

him? Are there people you have those complicated feelings about in real life?
9. *The Favourite:* Why do you think Sarah and Abigail would both want to take advantage of the queen's gout to fulfill their selfish pursuits for power? Do you think the queen ever did anything to deserve this exploitation?
10. *Crip Camp:* Upon seeing these people with disabilities fighting for their civil rights, and seeing how that led to the Americans with Disabilities Act of 1990, in what ways does that inspire you? How were their acts of protest effective in convincing the government to initiate the act?
11. Upon watching all these good examples, are there any you believe shouldn't be considered a good example?
12. Now, onto some personal takeaways. If you have a wheelchair or crutches at home from a prior injury, try going an entire day confined to them, going to a variety of places. If you don't have a wheelchair or crutches at home, invent a scenario where you stay on a couch/chair for a full twenty-four hours. What would you need to do to get help for simple everyday things? Both of these experiments will give you a better taste of what it's like for some people who live every day with a motor impairment condition.
13. What new/surprising knowledge did you pick up from reading this chapter?
14. What's the biggest misconception you learned about motor impairment?
15. And most importantly: How will you start to live differently having a new perspective on motor impairment?

Chapter 9: Mutism

My Personal Experience

Everyone I recall meeting throughout my life has for the most part spoken perfectly fine, and they never had any kind of anxiety disorder that would make them go silent in particular circumstances.

Growing up, I had many vacations to Disneyland and Walt Disney World. Now, what does Disney have to do with mutism? Well, the many costumed characters there, Mickey Mouse, Minnie Mouse, Goofy, Donald Duck, Pooh, Tigger, Pinocchio, Captain Hook, the Seven Dwarfs, the Genie, and many others, never spoke.

As a four-year-old, hugging the mascots was my favorite part of my family's Disney vacations, but I was always too afraid to approach the princesses, who strangely enough were allowed to talk. Looking at it now, I believe the power behind the fully costumed figures at theme parks has proven to be so timeless because gestures without words create a universal language anybody can understand.

That's probably why I loved the costumed characters so much; besides the fact that I was meeting all these cheerful characters from TV and movies, communication without the need to speak was meaningful for me in my speech delay.

Yes, I had speech delay, I was hardly talking by age two, so my parents had me take speech therapy even before I was diagnosed as autistic. Even now, the process of putting my thoughts into words is often too much of an ordeal for me to perform comfortably, so I often think I'm better off if I avoid most social situations, where I'm not struggling to think of ways to break any awkward silences in a conversation.

There's another issue that I discovered about myself just recently: in periods when I get especially nervous, anxious, depressed, or overwhelmed by others reprimanding me, I almost feel like I lose my ability to speak. Trying to put my thoughts into words from my mouth gets that much harder, to the point it sounds an awful lot like stammering; the more overwhelmed I get, the harder it is for me to speak. Yet the more comfortable I am in a social situation, the easier it is for me to speak freely.

There have even been some very rare occasions when my anxiety during a serious discussion reaches off-the-charts levels: my ability to speak would virtually be gone, and I would only be able to communicate by writing or typing. It's just something about the way my brain is wired that stops whatever part of it creates speech whenever those fearful emotions go haywire. I'm no scientist or doctor, so I can't explain how that works.

But my point is that when I learned about people with selective mutism while researching for this book, I immensely empathized with their conditions. In social situations, I do often struggle to think of anything to say, especially when it's just me and one other person by ourselves talking.

I now often wish that I had selective mutism, that way, I could have a good excuse to not have to talk to people. Writing stuff down is infinitely easier for me when communicating, because that way, I have the time to think about what to say before I put it on paper or my phone. That's probably why becoming an author was the easiest way for me to find work and make a difference in this world!

Quick Facts

There are two types of mutism:

- Neurogenic: Mutism caused by damage in the brain.
- Selective: An anxiety disorder where the person feels they cannot speak, except to a select few people. Less than 1% of children in the United States have this, and it's more common in females.

Selective Mutism can be broken down to:

- Elective: When the choice not to speak is intentional.
- Selective: When someone wants to speak but for some reason just can't.
- Total: When someone never speaks no matter the situation.

Types of neurogenic mutism can include:

- Apraxia: Irregular speech errors caused by a failure of motor function between the brain and articulators.
- Congenital High Airway Obstruction Syndrome: Birth without a larynx or airway
- Dysarthria: Physical deficits that affect speech.
- Aphasia: Caused by damage to the brain in areas that affect speech. This can be a result of injury or a disorder/disease. About 1 million people in the United States have this.

Aphasia can be broken down into:

- Fluent: Speech full of mostly nonsense words or disjointed phrases while speaking sentences.
- Nonfluent: Speech full of most words in sentences being omitted, such as the conjunctions.

Outside sources which can cause mutism include (but are not limited to:

- o Dementia
- o Developmental disorder
- o Medication
- o Physical disfigurement
- o Physical injury
- o Progressive disease
- o Seizure
- o Stroke
- o Surgery

The Film in Focus

Title	The Shape of Water
Director	Guillermo del Toro
Writer	Guillermo del Toro, Vanessa Taylor
Main Cast	Sally Hawkins, Richard Jenkins
Studio	Fox Searchlight Pictures
Country	United States
Release	22 December 2017
Runtime	2 hr. 3 min.

Synopsis

Elisa is a lonely mute woman who has scars on her neck and works as a janitor at a top-secret government facility. One night, one of the men, Mr. Strickland, brings a monumental discovery back from his Amazon excursion: an amphibious sea creature shaped like a man. A curious Elisa seems drawn to this amphibian man; she sneaks inside the chamber the beast is being kept in and takes out a hardboiled egg she brought to snack on. She teaches the creature the ASL sign for "egg," and he swiftly takes the egg, apparently having picked up the sign later on. Much later, after she and the amphibian man are given time to bond further, Elisa convinces her next-door neighbor, Giles, to help her free the amphibian man from the abusive Mr. Strickand.

The heist is successful, and the amphibian man is now living in her bathtub. She plans to wait until rain fills the city's canal so that it will open up to the ocean when she'll release the beast into the wild. Yet Strickland is investigating to figure out who stole his grand prize. When the amphibian man is released according to Elisa's plan, Strickland has all the pieces together of where and when Elisa will be with the creature.

At the scene in front of the canal, Strickland shows up and lands bullets on the two of them. Yet the amphibian man heals himself and jumps into the canal, carrying Elisa. Underwater, he kisses Elisa while he glows blue, and the scars on her neck turn into gills! Now she and the amphibian man can live happily ever after together beneath the waves.

The Film's Portrayal of the Disability

The culture depicted in this film, set in early 1960s Baltimore, is different from how most people today think of it. Back then, everyone just tolerated the unacceptable treatment toward minority groups, as demonstrated by a brief scene where Mr. Strickland's kids are watching *Mr. Magoo,* a cartoon that infamously mocked low-vision people.

Mr. Strickland, being a straight, White, nondisabled man, is the film's antagonist, and everything he says in Elisa's presence brims with insensitivity. At the end of the scene between Mr. Strickland,

Zelda, and Elisa in the bathroom, he says, "It's very nice chatting with you both," yet Elisa said nothing the whole time, and he didn't even care to notice. He does soon learn that she's mute, and decides to take advantage of her by sexually harassing her, saying that her inability to speak is a turn-on for him.

Elisa may not be able to speak, but she's still the only person her friend, Giles, can talk to, and she's the only one who willfully listens to her other friend, Zelda, rant about her husband and how much of a mess the other men in the facility leave for them to clean. Although the amphibian man is the first being she connects with by using her own method of communication.

Here is where the scars on Elisa's neck come in. While there is no way that cuts on the sides of her neck could have damaged her larynx to the point of permanent mutism, there's a deeper internet theory that explains her backstory: Elisa was part fish all along and the scars were underdeveloped gills. So the amphibian man didn't magically give her gills, he healed her gills so she could live back where she belongs. That furthermore explains why she has no voice, because, naturally, sea creatures can't talk.

Yet many from the disability community who have watched this movie took issue with the dream sequence where Elisa imagines herself singing "You'll Never Know (Just How Much I Love You)" to the amphibian man. The argument is that people with disabilities never dwell on those types of fantasies; blind people don't wish they could see, deaf people don't wish they could hear, autistic people don't wish they were cured, and mute people don't wish they could sing.

I don't think that narrow assumption is completely legitimate. In my experience, there have been so many times I wish I could find a cure for autism so I could communicate as easily as everybody else, there are still some days for me now when I hate the limitations of my autism. Therefore, this dream sequence in the movie checks out well for me.

There are some other controversies I've seen in this film's depiction of disability. One is making the disabled character an inhuman outsider. For that, I should also comment that she's still a good-natured human being who understands marginalized people and animals. Nothing about her actions in rescuing the amphibian man come off as overly sentimental, and her disability is never depicted as an obstacle for her to overcome. So she may be an outsider, but she's also portrayed with respect.

Though another controversy is the message that disabled people should stay with their own kind, away from all nondisabled people, as they'll only be accepted by those who couldn't judge them because they know no better anyway. Here's my rebuttal: Elisa finds people who love her and accept her in this society not built for disability accommodation, such as Giles and Zelda, not to mention it would have been insincere to depict a sudden 180-degree flip on society's acceptance of a disabled person.

With that said, *The Shape of Water* ought to be celebrated as a progressive step forward in disability representation. I mean, how many movies out there star a good-willed disabled character who expresses sexual desires within her first two minutes of introduction?

The Disability in Film History

These feature films below show ways this disability has been abused for the benefit of nondisabled people:

The Victim Trope

This includes *Johnny Got His Gun, The Diving Bell and the Butterfly, Extremely Loud and Incredibly Close,* and even the documentary *Life Itself,* which focuses on Roger Ebert's thyroid cancer. His entire jaw and mouth were removed by surgery, he had to be fed through a tube, and his method of communication was via computer, making this film critic legend look pitiful. Then in *Top Gun: Maverick,* Maverick reunites with his old friend Iceman, played by Val Kilmer, who in real life, has throat cancer. His character doesn't serve the story but was put in because Tom Cruise insisted that he be in the movie, and Kilmer's throat cancer happened to help make the audience cry, especially when his voice was recreated with AI software.

The Obstacle Trope

In *Planet of the Apes (1968),* George lands on a planet where apes evolved into the dominant species, and humans devolved into animal intelligence. George hurts his throat in an attack, which temporarily removes his speech and causes the other apes to assume he's no more intelligent than the other voiceless humans. Essentially, this monumental sci-fi classic promotes the belief that anyone who can't speak is like an animal. Though Disney's *The Little Mermaid (1989)* takes the cake as the worst offender of this trope, for it infamously teaches little girls that they should give up their voice to go marry a man they never even had a conversation with.

The Trauma Trope

In *Speak,* Kristen Stewart plays a teenage girl with severe social anxiety that often comes out in the form of selective mutism, which quickly leads to cruel treatment by the whole school. The reason she goes mute most of the time is because she got raped shortly before the school year started. Although the story means well in raising awareness for socially anxious teenagers, it also gives a bland black-and-white conclusion that trauma is always the cause of selective mutism. That's not the answer to how all cases start, especially with smaller children where the cause of their selective mutism can rarely be pinpointed.

The "Impossible to Communicate" Trope

In *Splash,* Madison the mermaid spends the first act unable to speak or even communicate, but then she spends an entire day in front of a TV and suddenly speaks quite well, turning her into an acceptable woman whom nobody would suspect is a sea creature. This theme is also found in *Pirates of the Caribbean: The Curse of the Black Pearl,* when it's said that a pirate on Captain Jack Sparrow's crew had his tongue cut out, and so he trained his parrot to speak for him. Both of these examples suggest that mute people can only communicate through supernatural means, or worse, through letting the TV put words into their mouths.

The Comic Relief Trope

Harpo Marx had famously never said a single word in any of the Marx Brothers movies he starred in because that was a massive component to his physical humor. The work of Harpo also could have been a major mode of inspiration for another beloved pop culture figure from the 1930s: Dopey in *Snow White and the Seven Dwarfs.* Although the silence did indeed work to the benefit of enhancing the physical humor, these two characters treat mute people like mere punchlines, especially when most of their humor comes from their inability to get across an idea with a character who can speak.

The Inspiration Trope

In *Gigot,* the title character is mute, and passersby on the street frequently laugh at him. As frustrating as it often gets that he never thinks to just use a pen and paper, he manages to communicate fine for the most part, particularly in using gestures to describe what people do in church. The problem with Gigot though is that he has no satisfactory conclusion to his troubles; his mutism is only there to make everyone feel sorry for him. Also, *The Theory of Everything* tells how Stephen Hawking overcame his ALS (which included the loss of his voice) and became among the most influential scientific minds in world history. The logic in this adaptation is... since Stephen Hawking in his suffering could communicate with a computer, anyone can do anything!

The Horror Trope

Frankenstein's monster is a classic example of disability used to generate fear; he never speaks, but only grunts and growls. When he was stitched together from numerous body parts acquired by corpses, he perhaps never got the part of the brain needed to generate speech. This famous horror flick doesn't treat with care what some audiences could be missing in their bodies, it just resorts to the lack of a voice to dehumanize the monster and make him scarier. That concept of silencing antagonists furthermore includes the silent Oddjob in *Goldfinger,* who is never treated as a character, he's just silent to make him less of a human being and more of a brick wall for James Bond to break down.

Also note the scary scene in *The Matrix* when Agent Smith says to Neo, "Tell me, Mr. Anderson, what good is a phone call if you're unable to speak?" The scene then quickly turns into a straight-up horror flick as Neo's mouth seals itself shut like glue. The impression there, between the line, the visual, and the emotion, is that not talking is scary.

*****

A non-speaking character can offer many powerful storytelling possibilities for this highly visual medium, which is why this treatment needs to be done delicately so that it respects those who are mute. Thankfully, some relatively recent movies have mastered the usage of this disability to advance their deeper themes in imaginative and respectful ways:

The Piano (1993) - *Australia*

Ada McGrath has no real idea why she hasn't spoken since age six, but regardless, she now communicates using sign language and slips of paper she wears around her neck. Though it's her treasured piano that gives her somewhat of a voice, which in turn drives the sexual tension between herself and another man. Soon, the conflict within this affair costs her a finger, and she ultimately parts from this majestic musical instrument. Yet that severance from the piano is just what Ada needs to finally feel motivated to start learning how to speak again, and with a new prosthetic finger.

Little Miss Sunshine (2006) - *United States*

Dwayne lives a selective mutism lifestyle and refuses to speak again until he receives his acceptance letter into Air Force training. It has been nine months since he began this vow, and he since then has only communicated by writing on a pad of paper. Then a harsh self-discovery gives him the start of the healing process he needed: he's colorblind, which means he can never become a pilot. As heartbroken as he is that his dream is vanquished, it needed to happen so that he would start communicating with his family again.

Song of the Sea (2014) -*Ireland*

Saoirse is a mute child with a selkie for a mother (a selkie is a mythological creature capable of changing from a seal to a human). Whenever Saoirse puts on a certain sealskin coat at night, she becomes a seal, thus, she could never afford to lose her seal coat, or she would fall ill. She does unfortunately part from the coat at one point, but then reunites with it, which opens up her ability to speak finally. In the end, she sacrifices her selkie powers to stay around her surviving family members, proving how this animated feature turns the "aquatic nonspeaking semi-human" trope into something much more deeply personal.

Us (2019) -*United States*

The tethered are doppelgangers that were part of a failed science experiment and now merely exist underground inside tunnels, helpless and without the ability to speak. But then there's Red, the tethered of Adelaide, who switched places with Adelaide and went on to live her life above the surface. When the parents find Red and think she's Adelaide, they believe she has selective mutism because of recent PTSD, but of course, that isn't the case.

Over time, Red learns human speech and starts her own family. Yet the other tethered continue to exist beneath the earth eating nothing but raw rabbits, and Adelaide over many years helps them raid the surface world together. *Us* is more than just a reflection of our darker selves, it reverses common thinking and proves how even these antagonistic tethered, like mute people, have their unique passions and want to live like their able-tongued counterparts.

Drive My Car (2021) -*Japan*

The actors of Yûsuke's play include a mute woman named Yoon-a, who is treated no differently than any typical speaker by the rest of the cast and crew. The main scene that explores Yoon-a's character doesn't focus as much on her disability, but more on her personality, as she signs while her husband interprets. Yet at the same time, the film never ignores the beauty of her mutism; toward the end, she gives a beautiful theatrical monologue all in Korean Sign Language, which is every bit as powerful as a theatrical monologue given by a verbal actor.

*****

So it should be no surprise that mutism is so rarely depicted in movies, and it's even rarer to see it done well. That's why making a truly phenomenal motion picture takes courage, and that's furthermore why we ought to praise whenever filmmakers fight against the fear of failure to tell a meaningful story. If that's done, the quality of diversity in storytelling should come naturally.

Discussion Questions

1. The film in focus, *The Shape of Water,* won the Academy Award for Best Picture in 2017. Do you think this deserved the award? Why or why not? Do you think its use of disability had anything to do with its win?
2. Do you think Elisa was really fully human and the scars on her neck just coincidentally look like gills? Or do you think that she was part fish all the time and that her lack of a voice was part of her being animalistic?
3. Why do you think Giles and Zelda are friends with Elisa? Do you think these friendships are genuine and healthy? Do they treat her as an equal?
4. In seeing how Mr. Strickland was sexually attracted to Elisa's inability to talk, why do you think he felt this way? Do you agree that silence is sexy? How do you think that sort of mindset would dehumanize and objectify those with the disability?
5. Watch a movie from the "Disability in Film History" section. Do you agree or disagree that the movie is a negative depiction of mutism? Why?
6. *The Piano:* Why do you think Ada stopped speaking when she was six? What was it, over time, that finally gave her the courage to learn to speak again? Did the loss of her finger have anything to do with it?
7. *Little Miss Sunshine:* Have you ever taken a "vow of silence?" If you have, what was it for? If not, what would you do it for? Do you think it's healthy to do something like this? Was Dwayne's vow of silence beneficial to his developmental health? Why or why not?
8. *Song of the Sea:* What was your reaction when you first heard Saoirse speak? What was your reaction when she

sang the "Song of the Sea" in the climax? How would a girl like Saoirse benefit from not being able to speak?
9. *Us:* Were you scared of the tethered? Did their inability to speak make you more scared of them? Since Red could just barely speak, were you scared of her? With that said, would you in a typical situation be scared of a person who can't talk, or maybe can't talk well?
10. *Drive My Car:* In a typical conversation, how often are you the one talking? If someone took away your voice and you could only communicate in writing or sign language, would your share of attention in the conversation be lower? How do you think the treatment of Yoon-a's character in this movie promotes the benefit of silence?
11. Upon watching all these good examples, are there any you believe shouldn't be considered a good example?
12. Now, onto some personal takeaways. Go an entire day without speaking. If you work from home all day, put yourself into a social situation where normally you'd have to talk. It could be a social outing or at the mall, but set aside twenty-four hours where you have to put in the effort to keep any words from escaping your mouth. How did you resort to communicating with others? What does this tell you about others who are mute?
13. What new/surprising knowledge did you pick up from reading this chapter?
14. What's the biggest misconception you learned about mutism?
15. And most importantly: How will you start to live differently having a new perspective on mutism?

Chapter 10: Deafness

My Personal Experience

Up until college, I didn't know any deaf or hard of hearing people, I only ever knew that people could be deaf because of a few times when a deaf actor would make a brief appearance on a TV show to teach kids a couple of ASL signs. Yet I knew nothing really about the deaf community until college when I was required to take three levels of a foreign language. Spanish in high school proved to be too difficult for me, and other spoken languages didn't look too promising, so I settled on American Sign Language, mainly because my best friend at the time studied it for his senior project and ended up loving it.

I ended up liking it; since I am a kinesthetic learner, and am someone who fidgets with my hands a lot, the language was a lot easier for me to learn than Spanish. I could memorize the ASL alphabet in basically a single day, and by the end of the week, I had understood enough basic signs to communicate with more advanced ASL students exclusively in that language.

Within a single year, I took the three levels of ASL across three quarters, and part of my assignment requirements was to fulfill hours of deaf community exposure. Among these exposures, I went to see a play of all deaf actors put on for an audience of all deaf people; it made me see how deaf performances can be just as dramatic in their own set of rules as compared to hearing performances. Deaf actors are much more visual in their body language, which opens opportunities for them to speak more deeply to the audience's feelings, which is harder to do verbally.

After getting my Associate's degree, I transferred to Arizona State University for my Bachelor's, where I had to take a fourth semester of a foreign language as a graduation requirement, and thankfully, they accepted ASL as a foreign language.

Now, that was the last of the ASL courses I took, yet there are still many signs that I can remember to this day, enough to make some basic gestures in the few times I've met other deaf people since then. In fact, an employment counselor of mine was deaf, and I was able to surprise her by revealing I know some ASL. Though my knowledge of it wasn't even close to enough for there to be a full conversation without an interpreter.

Overall, learning American Sign Language was an eye-opening exposure to a whole new community, which in turn helped me gain greater knowledge about a minority group I beforehand didn't know how to interact with. Without my ASL classes, I wouldn't have known that deaf people can have conversations across distances where hearing people would normally have to shout, or that holding a deaf person's hand is inconsiderate because it's essentially like holding their tongue, or that Cochlear Implants are such a hot topic of controversy because some deaf people believe it erases them of their identity.

Even today I'm learning new things about how deaf people can communicate. There's the Tadoma Speechreading Method, when the deaf person, usually deafblind, places their fingers gently on another's vocal cords to feel what they're saying. A deafblind advocate, Oscar Serma, also revolutionized a new touch-based system of deafblind communication: Pro-tactile ASL. Stuff like this proves how acceptance and inclusion of the deaf community are always advancing and improving with modern technologies, and there's an entire universe behind simple deafness that hearing people are unaware of.

Quick Facts

Here are the main types of conditions that affect hearing:

- Sensorineural: When either the inner ear or hearing nerve is damaged. (The most common type.)
- Conductive: When it's difficult for sounds to penetrate past the middle ear and into the inner ear, sometimes because of a foreign object. This is often treatable by surgery or medicine.
- Mixed: When symptoms include traits of both Sensorineural and Conductive Deafness.
- Auditory Neuropathy Spectrum Disorder: When damage to the ear can't distinguish sound for the brain to pick up.

Deafness can also be broken into:

- Unilateral: Deafness in one ear.
- Bilateral: Deafness in both ears.
- Symmetrical: Deafness of the same level in each ear.
- Asymmetrical: Deafness of different levels in each ear.
- Progressive: Deafness that worsens over time.
- Sudden: Deafness that happens quickly.
- Fluctuating: Deafness that gets better/worse over time.
- Stable: Deafness that stays the same over time.
- Pre-lingual: Deafness that happened before the person learned to talk.
- Post-lingual: Deafness that happened after the person learned to talk.
- Congenital: Deafness that's present at birth.
- Acquired/Delayed Onset: Deafness that happens later in a person's life.

Levels of deafness can be categorized as:

- Mild: A difficulty in hearing soft sounds.
- Moderate: When hardly any speech is heard whenever someone talks normally.
- Severe: When no speech is heard whenever someone talks normally.
- Profound: When only very loud sounds can be heard.

Some more important statistics:

- Hearing difficulty is more common with people who are older, from 6.3% among those aged 18–44 to 26.8% among those aged 65 and over.
- Men are nearly twice as likely to be deaf compared to women.
- Deafness is reported to be more common in people of Caucasian ethnicity. It's least common in people of African ethnicity.
- Less than 30% of people who could benefit from hearing aids have ever used them.
- Over 90% of deaf children are born to hearing parents. Of those parents, only 10% of them ever learn how to communicate with their deaf child using ASL.
- In 2019, nearly 6,000 newborn infants were diagnosed with permanent deafness.
- In 2017, it was estimated that only 53.3% of deaf people have jobs.
- By 2050, it's expected that 25% of the world's population will become hard of hearing.
- Contrary to what some hearing parents of deaf children want to think, only 30% to 40% of speech sounds can be lip-read.

The Film in Focus

Title	A Quiet Place
Director	John Krasinski
Writer	John Krasinski, Scott Beck
Main Cast	Millicent Simmonds, John Krasinski
Studio	Paramount Pictures
Country	United States
Release	6 April 2018
Runtime	1 hr. 30 min.

Synopsis

Our world has been overtaken by alien creatures, which humans have called, "Death Angels," they can't see but destroy anything or anyone that makes a sound. The Abbott family relies on sign language to communicate and has rigged their entire home so that nothing can make a sound. The father, Lee, has spent his time researching everything the media already speculated about the Death Angels, as well as modifying his daughter's Cochlear Implant. Yet that daughter, Regan, doesn't believe her father loves her.

The time eventually comes when the pregnant mother, Evelyn, breaks into labor pains while home alone. In her labor process, the kids get caught by one of the Death Angels outside on the farm, with themselves inside a truck. Lee approaches the scene and sacrifices himself to save Regan and her brother. The kids then reunite with their mother and newly born brother, and Regan sees the station her father set up to improve her CI. Here, she recognizes her father truly did love her after all.

The Death Angel then breaks into the room, but Regan gets an idea of how to stop it. She discovered from past encounters that the Death Angel hates the feedback sound of her Cochlear Implant, so she hooks it up onto the microphone, and the noise forces the hard outer shell on the monster's head to break open, Evelyn then fires a fatal bullet, killing the creature.

The Film's Portrayal of the Disability

While expressing her impressions about *A Quiet Place* on *Larry King Now*, deaf celebrity Marlee Matlin praised its representation of deafness, but felt the movie made a Cochlear Implant inaccurately act too much like a hearing aid, real Cochlear Implants create no feedback noise, nor are they interchangeable, as they are depicted in this film. Then again, the modifications Lee made to increase the implant's frequency intake perhaps caused it to create feedback noise, which could potentially explain the plot hole.

But even then, there's another minor detail that this movie gets wrong about deafness. Whenever the point of view shifts over to Regan while her Cochlear Implant is shut off, all ambiance sound completely goes away. This is not entirely accurate to what deaf people hear in real life, usually, they can hear tiny slivers of sound if it's loud enough, but based on my research, it's almost never complete silence like how it's depicted here. This is also found in other films about deaf people, including *Babel (2006)* and *CODA (2021)*.

Yet the overall production still massively benefits from casting a real deaf actress to play the deaf character. While arranging the cast, John Krasinski stated that he wanted a real deaf actress to play Regan, particularly one who grew up being the only deaf member of her family, just like Regan is. So Krasinski chose Millicent Simmonds, which ended up working for everyone, because Simmonds, along with an ASL advisor, taught the rest of the cast and crew sign language.

As far as the drama goes amongst the rest of the family, it strives to depict what it's like for a family where only one of them has a disability, and how the one with that disability seems to have the biggest insecurities of all. It could have been much better though, as the brother, father, and mother don't have much personality, which makes the family drama a bit insincere.

The closest to genuine the drama gets is Lee and Regan's argument over upgrading her implants. While the dialogue does clearly prioritize exposition over defining character, much of the context feels quite real to the issues between parents and their disabled children. Regan insists to her father that the custom implant won't work and that he'll never be able to "fix" her disability. It's typical for teenagers to think that their parents don't understand, and in many cases that's true, but imagine being deaf, blind, or autistic, while mom and/or dad doesn't have that corresponding disability.

But then comes the ending, while it's admittedly unrealistic that an average family could stop a supernatural force better than the military, it's vital to Regan's growth. She has to watch her father sacrifice himself to save her and her brother, and then afterward see all the work he's done in the basement, especially the whole station he set up to improve her Cochlear Implant. She realizes at last that although her father will never know what it's like being deaf in an all-hearing family, he still prioritized her safety and self-interest far beyond his own.

That advanced Cochlear Implant likewise helps save the family from the Death Angel when she uses it to create enough feedback noise to open the creature's head so mom could kill it. So the family truly did work together to save themselves, all because of what made Regan unique in the family.

It's amazing how a movie released before the COVID-19 pandemic miraculously predicted that our noisy culture would become our downfall without the unsung heroes, such as those with disabilities. *A Quiet Place* offers representation beyond what audiences would expect from an independently produced horror movie, where the most underappreciated people groups, which includes the one deaf person in an all-hearing family, have the tightest grasp of the problems in dark times.

The Disability in Film History

While it's quickly become one of the most common disabilities portrayed in media, deafness has still been largely misrepresented with a plethora of stereotypes.

The Obstacle Trope

In *Mr. Holland's Opus*, Mr. Holland struggles to connect with his deaf son, and that turmoil treats the disability as a tragic fate for a boy to live through, which furthermore becomes an obstacle in the path to Mr. Holland's profession. Likewise, a subplot in *Babel* focuses on the miserable sob story of a heartbroken deaf girl who can't enjoy the pleasures her peers get to enjoy. Her disability is never celebrated, it just gets in her way.

The Victim Trope

The Netflix movie *Hush* depicts a young woman made permanently deaf-mute due to bacterial meningitis, which is only there to worsen her predicament as a masked killer begins to stalk her in her own house. Plus, Chief Bromden from *One Flew Over the Cuckoo's Nest* feigns deafness for most of the film, which causes the other residents and staff to bully him until he reveals he's not really "deaf and dumb." And while *The Family Stone* attempts to disapprove of any mistreatment toward deaf people, it features a deaf gay family member, Thad, whose only purpose is to start family tension without any real redemption seen on his end.

Hearing People Practicing Dominance Over Deaf People

In *Children of a Lesser God,* James is a speech teacher at a deaf school who teaches deaf students how to speak. Many of the students there can lipread, but Sarah, a young deaf woman who works as a custodian there, cannot (and will not) lipread. James develops a romantic attraction toward Sarah and wants to help her communicate, but she prefers to be herself. But she still admits that she doesn't even fully know herself, so of course, it takes her submission to a hearing man, one whose career is all about potentially curing deaf students, to help her discover herself. This is a fine example of cinematic masculinity where the man practices dominance in the relationship.

The Superhuman Trope

Makkari of *Eternals* made history as cinema's first-ever deaf superhero, which is made even more amazing by the fact that she's played by a deaf woman named Lauren Ridloff. However, the treatment of her character isn't about raising awareness or empowering a group of people, it's actually about using the disability to make her an awesome superhuman. It's not appropriate to diminish the struggles of a person's disability just to turn their lack of vision, hearing, etc. into a superpower.

The Dependency Trope

In *CODA,* Ruby wants to leave her all-deaf family to pursue an education in music, yet her parents insist she stays since she's their free ASL interpreter. These deaf parents are depicted as being nothing but awful human beings who manipulate and take advantage of their daughter and try to appear helpless without the help of someone who can hear. In another similar case of making deaf people look inferior to hearing people, *The Miracle Worker (1962),* makes Helen Keller's condition look like an absolute tragedy until Anne Sullivan arrives to teach her how to communicate. In many scenes of her alone with Helen, Anne speaks to her verbally, most likely so the audience could understand her, even though in real life this would be a great insult toward a deaf person.

The Plot Convenience Trope

There are two examples of this from two recent major blockbusters. The first is *Godzilla vs. Kong,* which features deaf actress Kaylee Hottle playing a deaf girl, the only person in the movie who can communicate with the giant ape by using ASL. The second is in *Dune (2021)* when Paul and his mother manage to escape capture because one of the guards is deaf. Each of these examples dehumanizes deafness by turning them into plot conveniences for the hearing characters.

The Comic Relief Trope

Instances of this are very rare, but it has happened a few times before; *See No Evil, Hear No Evil* has made fun of both deafness and blindness. Deafness also has been used as an insult a number of times in the *Back to the Future* trilogy, especially in the second one, when Marty McFly says to Griff, "What are you? Deaf and stupid?" This has happened as well in *Willy Wonka and the Chocolate Factory;* when asked how he makes the everlasting gobstoppers, Wonka just says, "I'm a trifle deaf in this ear. Speak a little louder next time."

*****

Though plenty of good examples in recent memory have positively represented the community:

There Will Be Blood (2007) - *United States*

After striking it rich with oil, the unthinkable hits Daniel Plainview: an oil explosion causes permanent damage to his son's eardrums. Nothing from there could stop the path Daniel's son takes: he learns ASL, gets married, and plans to leave his father's business to start his own in Mexico. Daniel, in his fury, challenges his son to speak verbally rather than sign to him, and surprisingly, he does manage to verbalize some words despite his deafness. Paul Thomas Anderson's dim cautionary tale about the rise of Industrial America illustrates the irreversible damage greed does to a father who neglects his son's health.

Barfi! (2012) -*India*

Barfi's deafness consequently ignites his courage as he constantly flees authority by his execution of stunts akin to Charlie Chaplin and Buster Keaton. Yet in the moments he's finally caught, the law enforcement shows no respect toward his disability. But that's okay because Barfi has other methods of communication, such as pantomime to express his love for a girl. Though his sympathy toward women is made complete when he gets to know Jhilmil, who has autism. Barfi's adventures prove how even a disabled person's capacity to love, whether for another disabled woman or for a nondisabled one, can grow and mature in the same way as a neurotypical human.

A Silent Voice (2016) -*Japan*

Unlike other stories about bullying, *A Silent Voice* takes the bully's point of view as well as the victim's. Back in sixth grade, Shôya had a deaf girl named Shoko in his class, and throughout the year, he ripped out her hearing aids over and over, which scars her to the point she has to leave the school. Now as a teenager, Shôya feels indescribably guilty over his old ways, and it reaches the point when he plans to commit suicide. Meanwhile, Shoko also hates herself to the point she genuinely believes she's better off dead. This is such a humble, vulnerable antibullying film that can help kids with a disability learn to love themselves.

Sound of Metal (2020) -*United States*

Ruben Stone has played drums in a heavy metal band for so long that he's now losing his hearing... to the point of permanent deafness. He has no choice but to accept this awful new normal, and the deaf community he joins over time helps him discover what it truly means to be deaf, and he in turn feels more comfortable about this new normal. *Sound of Metal* gives a hard message: Because Ruben couldn't appreciate life outside of the noise, his ears had to fail him so he could grow into a more appreciative man.

A Quiet Place Part II (2021) -*United States*

This sequel's originally planned release date was May 2020, but once COVID-19 took over the globe a mere months earlier, John Krasinski had to push the release date. Yet the delay worked to his advantage because in May 2021, *A Quiet Place Part II* expanded into the apocalyptic wasteland that feels not a whole lot different than society in quarantine. Regan is still the movie's only deaf character, and still holds the key to stopping the Death Angels. There are more people that the remaining members of the Abbott family come across, and they're all suffering from the plague of Death Angels. Yet people like Regan, despite her age, prove to be vital components that will help society restore itself.

*****

During the production of this book, *CODA* won the 2022 Oscar for Best Picture, which is a major step forward in the film industry that will lead to better portrayals of the deaf community and greater job opportunities for those people. There have been other ways filmmakers in recent years have come to a closer understanding of the community, the depiction of ASL in *Godzilla vs. Kong* is surprisingly not far off, as some apes in history were taught many ASL signs, such as a gorilla named Michael, who knew over 600 ASL signs and could tell the tragic story of how he lost his parents. It's great that Hollywood sees the beauty in such a visual language, even in the times they're not portraying the community quite right. Deafness has miraculously become one of the rare disabilities that's become mainstream and is for the most part celebrated.

Discussion Questions

1. The film in focus, *A Quiet Place*, has gained massive financial success, even with the second movie coming out during the COVID-19 pandemic. What do you think contributed to the success of these movies? Did their use of a deaf actress have anything to do with it?
2. Looking at the types of deafness at the start of this chapter, which one do you think Regan has? What evidence makes you reach that conclusion? How does that specific categorization of deafness affect the treatment of her character?
3. Does the ending celebrate Regan as a person or the mere fact that she conveniently had the tool necessary to stop the monster?
4. Were you convinced that Lee truly did love his daughter? What made you convinced of that? Or what didn't convince you of that?
5. Watch a movie from the "Disability in Film History" section. Do you agree or disagree that the movie is a negative depiction of deafness? Why?
6. *There Will Be Blood:* Think of any significant trauma that has happened within your family. How did you get out of it in the end? Were you closer or further apart as a result? How do you think this conflict translates to families where one member of it is deaf but the others aren't? How is it similar to or different than in this movie?
7. *Barfi!:* Is the title character for this movie how you typically think of deaf people? What types of character quirks would you often expect from seeing a deaf person on screen? In what ways does this movie defy those stereotypes?

8. *A Silent Voice:* Have you been bullied back in school? Have you ever bullied a specific student? How do the victimization and guilt on both ends currently make you feel? Are your feelings similar to Shôya's and Shoko's suicidal behaviors? How does that make you want to treat people with a disability like deafness differently?
9. *Sound of Metal:* How would you feel if you lost your hearing and could never listen to your favorite genre of music again? Or if you play a musical instrument and lost your hearing, what else would you put your hope in? How would you say your response is similar to the way Ruben handles his deafness in this movie?
10. *A Quiet Place Part II:* Thinking back to any emotional turmoil your family or community has been through lately, how have the unsung heroes come out? How has their age or disability worked to their advantage?
11. Upon watching all these good examples, are there any you believe shouldn't be considered a good example?
12. Now, onto some personal takeaways. Next time you watch a movie you've never seen before, turn the volume off. Only rely on the closed captions throughout the entire movie. What did you notice about this experience that you couldn't notice with the sound on?
13. What new/surprising knowledge did you pick up from reading this chapter?
14. What's the biggest misconception you just learned about the deaf community?
15. And most importantly: How will you start to live differently having a new perspective on deafness?

Conclusion

"My advice to other disabled people would be, concentrate on things your disability doesn't prevent you doing well, and don't regret the things it interferes with. Don't be disabled in spirit as well as physically."

- Stephen Hawking

As you can probably see by now, disability misrepresentation in film is very different now than it was a hundred years ago. There may be more understanding of the struggles people go through, but there is now a new form of mistreatment. It consists of internet posts where nondisabled people look at a disabled girl and say to one another, "Think you have a hard life? Look at her! Now stop complaining!" Or maybe, "Because this boy without arms can put on his shoes in the morning, you can accomplish anything you put your mind to!" Such slogans suggest that anyone with a disability shouldn't be expected to do normal everyday tasks, and objectifies them to being not people, but models on a motivational poster.

Watch any interview about disabled people on YouTube, and you'll find the comment section is full of phrases such as, "oh s/he has such a beautiful heart!" "I would love to be your friend!" "What a powerful mother she is for sticking with the child!" "How wonderful to see the classmates be so supportive!" While I prefer reading these over, "People like him are better off dead, lol" a danger still exists behind these well-meaning heartfelt comments. It merely dehumanizes the person with a disability to being nothing more than a beacon of Jesus-level holiness who only is a comparison point for nondisabled folk, not to be human beings in their own right.

I know from first-hand experience that people on the autism spectrum are just as multi-dimensional as anyone else, I've known some with ASD who were mean, disrespectful, and rude due to some past trauma, but I've also met other teens with developmental disorders who were total sweethearts, always coming up to hug me! Just like the good movie examples you've seen throughout this book, there are good and bad people with disabilities, and they all have their own backstories that make them more than just disabled people.

With that said, any piece of media, be it fictional or nonfictional, can easily skew the facts to make a disabled person as righteous or as profane as the director wants. Interview subjects could always be lying or reading off cue cards, and certain parts of what they say could be left out. Not to mention there are many times when talk of helping people with disabilities is focused on the nondisabled folk rather than letting the people with disabilities speak for themselves. That's why you must always maintain a critical eye whenever you come across any disability-based media, be it an interview, promotional video, TV show, or movie.

So when it comes to the movies you watch in your leisure, I leave you with this: Watch content outside your comfort zone. You never know when a new discovery will become another top ten favorite movie of yours. Before college, I wouldn't have watched *Amadeus, American Beauty, Life of Pi, The Shape of Water,* or *Us.* Without my film degree, I might still see Pixar as artistic perfection and would never stretch my familiarity in the world of movies.

Since I came to discover what makes a great movie, I've begun to take steps to undo how I let morally poor media corrupt my thinking toward people with disabilities. The first step I took was purging any badly made movies from my Blu-ray shelf, including the *Harry Potter* series and *Men in Black,* as much as it disheartened me to do so. Now instead of *Men in Black,* my Dad and I watch *Terminator 2: Judgment Day* together. Now instead of Hogwarts, I enjoy the fantasy worlds of Middle Earth and *Avatar: The Last Airbender.*

Closing Questions

1. Go back to your list of 10-20 favorite movies from the intro chapter.
    - Did you see any of those movies mentioned anywhere in this book? Look in the index if you can't remember whether you did.
    - Were you sad/glad/mad about what you saw said about those movies from your list in this book?
2. Which disability do you feel most drawn to learn about?
    - What movies mentioned in this book can help you to learn more about that disability?
3. I know it's hard to tell which media has positive representation. So here are some questions to test the quality of how a movie or TV show portrays a disability:
    - Look at the very first frame and very last frame of the media piece, who or what is the focus?
    - What emotions are you made to feel? Are you left feeling motivated or discouraged?
    - Are there action steps taken to help the real problems the person with a disability is facing?
    - How realistic is this supposedly real-life event? Are there things that prove it's all staged? For instance, if a reality TV show features someone knocking on another's door, is everyone answering fully dressed in nice outfits with shoes and makeup on, despite the fact they supposedly weren't expecting anyone to come to their door?
4. Need a place to start in exploring new movies? Maybe watch everything that won the Best Picture Oscar, and pull out perhaps your ten favorite ones.

Appendix

Modern Examples of Disability Acceptance

- Urinals are closer to the ground at the end of the row in public bathrooms to help dwarfs and wheelchair users.
- Automatic door openers, ramps, and disability accessible parking spots and bathrooms are mandatory by state.
- English dubs are made for foreign films and TV shows, which can help English speakers with dyslexia.
- The late 19th century's "Ugly Laws" are no longer in effect.
- Organizations such as the Wheaton Center for Faith and Disability are helping schools and churches become disability welcoming.
- The conjoined twins Abby and Brittany Hensel have happy careers as grade school teachers and are loved by their community in New Brighton, Minnesota.
- Charla Nash, the woman whose face and hands were ripped up well beyond recognizability by her friend's pet chimpanzee, is still alive and well today, met with immense sympathy by the internet. Her story also partially inspired Jordan Peele's *Nope*.
- During the COVID-19 pandemic, Millicent Simmonds made masks to help deaf people with lipreading.
- Gary Sinise continues to be an advocate for the Disabled American Veterans Organization.
- Certain celebrities, such as Lupita Nyong'o and Chris Pratt, have openly taken responsibility for the times they misrepresented people with disabilities.
- TV shows such as *Family Guy* have cast people with disabilities to provide voices for disabled characters, including Marlee Matlin or Andrea F. Friedman (who has Down Syndrome).

Evidence We Still Have a Long Way to Go

- Some people still believe that vaccines cause autism.
- Some people still believe that various diseases (including autism) are curable by bleach and electroshock therapy.
- Infomercial products are being made with disability aids in mind (such as an egg-cracker meant to help people with arthritis, or a shoe horn on a stick that can help people with back problems), yet are advertised to the general public.
- Animals and pets with physical disfigurement (such as Tardar Sauce... AKA "Grumpy Cat") are still made into memes and headliner articles meant to shock readers.
- There have been cases of some users on TikTok pretending to have various disorders, such as Tourette's.
- There are still thousands of people who spend years and years cooped up in their homes and never leave for several reasons, be it an inability to walk, obesity, PTSD, or any other disability-related obstacle.
- Kids and adults with disabilities are still being bullied by students, teachers, bosses, coworkers, family, and others.
- The ways those people with disabilities are bullied continue to grow more horrific. One streamer on Twitch, Sweet Anita, who has severe Tourette's, reported how she once was beaten by bullies until she was unconscious. Up until she gained popularity on Twitch, she was agoraphobic and avoided people altogether.
- As you have read in this book, there's still way more negative representation than positive representation of disabilities in movies.

Underrepresented Disabilities in Film

Down Syndrome is reportedly the most common genetic disorder, and I've met several people who have it. Yet, I've only ever seen one movie that features Down Syndrome: *The Peanut Butter Falcon,* where the main actor, Zack Gottsagen, has Down Syndrome in real life. While this should be seen more in movies, the lack of Down Syndrome representation is understandable because no actor without Down Syndrome could pass as looking like they have it.

Tourette's Syndrome, which I've only seen in *Motherless Brooklyn* and has all sorts of misconceptions about it that warrant the need to be represented in movies more. For instance, the disorder does not universally mean a person is always swearing uncontrollably, some people just have tiny unnoticeable tics such as rapid eye movement.

Stuttering, which you may not see that often in the real world anyway, but in film, it tends to be present either to inspire audiences (such as in *The King's Speech)*, create a memorable character (such as in *Do the Right Thing)*, or associate them with evil (such as DJ from *Star Wars: The Last Jedi).* So this could use better quality representation.

Lisping, which you may instantly recognize in the hilarious "mawwage" scene in *The Princess Bride* and Sid the sloth in the *Ice Age* series. There's also a running gag in *The Muppet Movie* when Kermit the Frog repeats the word "myth" over and over until a lady suddenly appears saying, "yeth?" (Get it? Kermit sounded like he just said "miss" with a lisp!) So, as you can see, this is another disability that is negatively represented.

Conjoined Twins in *Chained for Life (1952), The Addams Family (1991),* and *Big Fish.*

Polydactyly in *The Princess Bride.*

Gynecomastia in *Fight Club.*

Hypertrichosis in *Fur: An Imaginary Portrait of Diane Arbus* and *Nightmare Alley (2021).*

Underdeveloped Thumbs in *Monsters vs. Aliens.*

Spasmodic Dysphonia was the mode of inspiration for Red's voice in *Us.*

A fantasy of a ten-year-old boy aging four times faster than average (which is a lot like Progeria) is used in *Jack (1996).*

Morbius invents a fake Blood Disease to give the guy his vampire superpowers.

Oscar Bait and Disabilities

"Oscar bait" is a term known well in the film community when describing movies that exist for the sole purpose of winning awards. They often follow a predictable checklist of components that Academy voters seem to like. Those elements could include a period setting, relevant issues about race and gender, a famous actor transforming into a historical figure, anything about the performing arts, or anything involving disability:

- *The Elephant Man*
- *On Golden Pond*
- *Amadeus*
- *Children of a Lesser God*
- *Fatal Attraction (1987)*

- *Moonstruck*
- *Rain Man*
- *Born on the Fourth of July*
- *My Left Foot*
- *Awakenings (1990)*
- *Scent of a Woman*
- *Schindler's List*
- *What's Eating Gilbert Grape*
- *The Piano*
- *Forrest Gump*
- *Braveheart*
- *Mr. Holland's Opus*
- *Breaking the Waves*
- *The English Patient*
- *Shine*
- *Good Will Hunting*
- *Saving Private Ryan*
- *Girl, Interrupted*
- *A Beautiful Mind*
- *I Am Sam*
- *The Lord of the Rings*
- *The Aviator*
- *Million Dollar Baby*
- *Ray*
- *Babel*
- *The Prestige*
- *The Diving Bell and the Butterfly*
- *Lars and the Real Girl*
- *There Will Be Blood*
- *The Curious Case of Benjamin Button*
- *Avatar*

- *127 Hours*
- *Black Swan*
- *The King's Speech*
- *A Separation*
- *Extremely Loud and Incredibly Close*
- *The Iron Lady*
- *Silver Linings Playbook*
- *The Wolf of Wall Street*
- *The Theory of Everything*
- *Still Alice*
- *The Revenant*
- *The Greatest Showman*
- *The Shape of Water*
- *Three Billboards Outside Ebbing, Missouri*
- *Wonder*
- *The Ballad of Buster Scruggs*
- *The Favourite*
- *Joker*
- *Sound of Metal*
- *CODA*
- *Drive My Car*
- *The Father*
- *Nightmare Alley (2021)*
- *Cyrano (2022)*
- *The Banshees of Inisherin (2022)*

Notice how very few of these examples feature a disabled actor playing a disabled character, which besides depriving the opportunity for those same people to get jobs, ultimately advances the Hollywood and social mindset that disabled people exist so that "normal" people can profit off of them.

How Media Can Be Dangerous: A Case Study

You may argue, "It's just a movie! Don't take it so seriously!" And yes, I understand. I too love being entertained by a movie or TV show on a lazy Saturday night. But I believe that taking in too much poorly produced media can have a significant negative impact on who you become, especially when watched at a young age. I know because it happened to me.

Back in my middle-school years, I spent way too many hours watching the Nickelodeon sitcom *Drake & Josh,* which was about two very different teenage boys who became stepbrothers. Drake was the cool kid every boy wishes they could be, whereas Josh was the awkward overweight loser who enjoyed stupid stuff like magic tricks and sniffing cheese. Drake led a rock band, had a new girlfriend each week, hardly ever suffered any consequences for his irresponsible behavior (unless Josh was involved), and won every competition he partook in (unless his little sister Megan interfered). On the other hand, Josh was the victim of harassment and insults, especially by unattractive women, and only won anything if he did it with Drake.

Naturally, I took the comparison to heart. I wanted to be like Drake, but in actuality, I was like Josh. So on my first day of ninth grade, I set a goal of getting a girlfriend before the year ended.

Here was the problem though: at the time I had no friends or social group, and because of my autism, personal space and civil conversation were not my best skills. My idea of flirting with girls was teasing them and sneaking up behind them to startle them—you know, middle school boy type of humor.

This behavior of mine brought me into the vice principal's office on three separate occasions, and one of those times, I almost got suspended. Thankfully I learned that what I was doing was wrong, but *Drake & Josh* left negative ideas that I haven't yet eliminated.

Every one of the show's fifty-five episodes and three direct-to-TV movies contained at least one negative stereotype toward a minority group, be it race, gender, or ability, and this is not even counting the other teen sitcoms of the time that I watched. *Hannah Montana, iCarly, The Suite Life of Zack and Cody, Zoey 101,* and many other similar shows of the time collectively threw insulting jabs at every disability imaginable.

So I hope to reverse the damage I did to myself in middle school, which makes writing this book so valuable to me. I'd like to do the same for others in their thinking about the media.

Acknowledgments

I would like to give a thank you to each of the following for reviewing the content of this book to ensure that what I'm saying is accurate and respectful of the various disability communities:

- Weston Ambrose
- Josh Goldschmid
- Barbara Hung
- Keith Krell
- Christopher McMillan
- Ron Ovadenko
- Jenn Ramirez Robson
- Roy Simpson
- Thomas Simpson

I also would like to thank my editor/mother, Patty Pacelli, who helped me through this laborious process of organizing my research and explaining it in a way that makes sense. Likewise, I would like to thank my father, Lonnie Pacelli, for whom of which the making of this book would not be possible, seeing how he suggested the idea of it in the first place. I also want to thank Andrew Faulds for referencing me to the Wheaton Center for Faith and Disability, which is mentioned in this book, Alexander James for reviewing the cover for this book, and of course, my dog Bella, for being my personal co-worker and cheerleader as I worked on this from home.

Notes

AnthonyPadilla. "I spent a day with people w/ DOWN SYNDROME" *YouTube,* 16 Mar 2022.

AnthonyPadilla. "I spent a day with SWEET ANITA: 'When Tourettes is Reality'" *YouTube,* 22 Apr 2022.

"A to Z of Disabilities and Accommodations." *Job Accommodation Network.*

Bolin, Carrie; Orlando, Jordie R.; Paul, Rachel. "Ripley's Believe It or Not! 100 Best Believe It or Not Stories." *Random House Books,* 2019.

"Disablism and ableism." *Scope.*

Gold, Jenni. "CinemAbility: The Art of Inclusion." *Gold Pictures,* 5 October 2018.

Hardwick, Lamar. "Diversity and Disability in the Church." *BioLogos,* 14 Oct 2021.

Hardwick, Lamar. "Disability and the Church." *InterVarsity Press,* 2021.

Harrison, Ashley J; Stronach, Sheri; Yu, Luodi. "Public knowledge and stigma of autism spectrum disorder: Comparing China with the United States" *National Library of Medicine,* 27 Apr 2020.

prattprattpratt. "Instagram does this thing where it mutes all the videos it shows and forces you to turn on the volume in order to hear them..." *Instagram,* 4 May 2017.

Pulver, Andrew. "Lupita Nyong'o apologises after Us 'evil' voice disability row." *The Guardian,* 1 Apr 2019.

Rust, John. "Tod Browning's 'Freaks': The Sideshow Cinema." *Warner Home Video,* 10 Aug 2004.

Schneider, Steven Jay; Smith, Ian Haydn. "1001 Movies You Must See Before You Die." *Barron's Educational Series, Inc.,* 2013 (5th Edition).

Schweik, Susan; Wilson, Robert. "Ugly Laws." *Eugenics Archive*, 5 Feb 2015.
Stanton, Greg. "Some Call Them... Freaks." *HBO,* 1981.
Sweet Anita. "It's just dawned on me that I was a social phobic recluse, agoraphobic, home educated and alone for 25 years. I mostly developed social my skills in the past 5 years! Most people learn how to interact with others since birth. If I can go from no friends to thousands in that time-" *Twitter,* 17 Aug 2020.
"What is Limb Length Discrepancy (LLD)?" *Nationwide Children's.*
"Wheaton Center for Faith and Disability." *Wheaton College.*

Blindness

"10 little-known facts about blindness." *Perkins School for the Blind.*
Ackland, Peter; Bourne, Rupert; Resnikoff, Serge. "World blindness and visual impairment: despite many successes, the problem is growing." *NCBI,* 2017.
"AFI's 10 Top 10." *American Film Institute,* 2008.
"AFI's 100 Years... 100 Cheers." *American Film Institute,* 2005.
"AFI's 100 Years... 100 Heroes & Villains." *American Film Institute,* 2003.
"AFI's 100 Years... 100 Laughs." *American Film Institute,* 2000.
"AFI's 100 Years... 100 Movies – 10th Anniversary Edition." *American Film Institute,* 2007.
"AFI's 100 Years... 100 Movies." *American Film Institute,* 1998.
"AFI's 100 Years... 100 Passions." *American Film Institute,* 2002.
"Avoidable Blindness." *Operation Eyesight.*
Award Productions. "Blind Baseball." *YouTube,* 18 Aug 2009.
"Blindness Statistics." *NFB,* Jan. 2019.
"City Lights (1931)." *Filmsite.*

Fleming, Seán. "7 smart tech developments for people who are blind or have low vision." *Microsoft*, 8 Aug 2019.

Henkler, Ed. "Braille Alternative is ELIA Frames." *The Blind Guide*, 25 Apr. 2018.

Larson, Jennifer. "What Do Blind People See?" *Healthline*, 20 Nov. 2019.

"Low Vision and Legal Blindness Terms and Descriptions." *AFB*.

Moallem, Ted. "Deafblind Users of Tadoma Speechreading Method." *YouTube*, 28 Aug 2011.

"Randolph Sheppard Vending Facility Program." *U.S. Department of Education*.

"Reviewing the Disability Employment Research on People who are Blind or Visually Impaired: Key Takeaways." *AFB*.

"Statistical Snapshots from the American Foundation for the Blind." *AFB*.

Thaler, Lore. "Echolocation may have real-life advantages for blind people: An analysis of survey data." *PubMed*, May 2013.

Vance, Jeffrey. "City Lights." *Chaplin: Genius of the Cinema*, Nov. 2003.

Little People

Dunkin, Mary Anne. Bhargava, Hansa D., MD. "Dwarfism." *WebMD*, 8 Sept 2020.

Guardian, The. "Being a Little Person in America: 'We're still treated as less than human.'" *YouTube*, 16 Oct 2019.

Kugler, Mary, RN. "The Most Common Types of Dwarfism." *Very Well Health*, 3 Nov 2021.

"LPA issues statement to abolish the "m" word." *Little People of America*, Sept 2015.

"Spondyloepiphyseal dysplasia congenita." *Medline Plus*, 18 Aug 2020.

"The Doll Family: Little People in Vaudeville by David Soren." *The University of Arizona: The American Vaudeville*, 2021.

Villines, Zawn; Luo, Elaine K., MD. "All you need to know about dwarfism." *Medical News Today*, 9 Dec 2017.

Facial Disfigurement

Blatty, David. "Joseph Merrick." *Biography,* 10 Nov 2014.

David Lynch Collection. "Making of The Elephant Man - David Lynch, Mel Brooks, John Hurt, Freddie Francis, Jonathan Sanger." *YouTube,* 28 Jul 2021.

Fisher, John Hayes; Walker, Emma. "The True Story of Joseph Merrick: 'The Elephant Man'." *BBC,* 27 May 1997.

Hollywood Suite. "How David Lynch's The Elephant Man Changed The Oscars Forever." *YouTube,* 16 Apr 2018.

"IMDb Top 250 Movies" *IMDb.*

Mullin, Gemma. "THE BOY WITH TWO FACES 'Miracle' boy born with extremely rare condition that gave him 'two faces' defies odds to celebrate 13th birthday." *The Sun,* 6 Jun 2017.

"Neurofibromatosis." *Medline Plus*, 29 Sept 2016.

"Proteus syndrome." *Medline Plus,* 18 Aug 2020.

"Skin Conditions by the Numbers." *AAD,* 2021.

"The most common forms of facial disfigurement." *Let's Face It,* 2019.

"Treacher Collins syndrome." *Medline Plus,* 18 Aug 2020.

Tunzelmann, Alex von. "The Elephant Man: close to the memoirs but not the man." *The Guardian*, 10 Dec 2009.

Autism

Associated Press. "'RAIN MAN' - THE ROLE HOFFMAN ALMOST QUIT." *Desert News,* 29 Dec 1988.

Brian Linehan's City Lights. "Dustin Hoffman Interview 1988 Brian Linehan's City Lights." *YouTube*, 16 Sept 2015.

cisio64123. "Siskel & Ebert - Rain Man." *YouTube*, 9 Jul 2009.

"Data & Statistics on Autism Spectrum Disorder." *Centers for Disease Control and Prevention.*

"Get to know the real Rain Man: Kim Peek." *Aruma.*

Norton, Amy. "Young adults with autism lag in school, work." *Chicago Tribune*, 15 May 2012.

Rensin, David. "Barry Levinson on the Making of 'Rain Man.'" *Rolling Stone*, 12 Jan 1989.

Roux, Anne M., Shattuck, Paul T., Rast, Jessica E., Rava, Julianna A., and Anderson, Kristy, "A. National Autism Indicators Report: Transition into Young Adulthood." *Philadelphia, PA: Life Course Outcomes Research Program, A.J. Drexel Autism Institute, Drexel University,* 2015.

Sarris, Marina. "A LOST GENERATION: GROWING UP WITH AUTISM BEFORE THE 'EPIDEMIC'." *Interactive Autism Network*, 25 Jul 2017.

"Stimming." *Merriam-Webster*, 2022.

"Then and Now: A Look at Autism Over the Last 20 Years." *SARRC.*

"What are the 5 Types of Autism?" *Integrity Inc*, 2019.

Limb Loss/Difference

"Amniotic Band Syndrome." *Boston Children's Hospital*, 2005-2022.

Bradford, Terry; McGimpsey, Grant. "Limb Prosthetics Services and Devices." *Worcester Polytechnic Institution.*

"Gary Sinise." *Association of the United States Army*, 2021.

"Hanhart syndrome." *National Center for Advancing Translational Sciences*, 3 Mar 2015.

Lewis, Rebecca. "Saving Private Ryan's harrowing 23-minute opening scene cost $12 million to make." *Metro*, 11 Jul 2018.
"Limb Loss and Limb Difference: Facts, Statistics, & Resources." *Hanger Clinic*, 1 Apr 2022.
"Limb Loss in the U.S." *Amputee Coalition*, 2014.
"Limb Loss." *Medline Plus*, 29 Jul 2021.
"Prosthetic Leg Cost | Factors that Affect Prosthetic Leg Price." *Scheck & Siress*, 2022.
Shores, Jaimie Troyal, M.D. "Amputation." *John Hopkins Medicine*, 2022.
"Thrombocytopenia-absent radius syndrome." *Medline Plus*, 8 Sept 2020.
"Vascular Diseases." *Medline Plus*, 21 Apr 2022.

Mental Illnesses

AnthonyPadilla. "I spent a day with MULTIPLE PERSONALITIES (Dissociative Identity Disorder)." *YouTube*, 4 Mar 2020.
Bhandari, Smitha, MD. "Causes of Mental Illness." *WebMD*, 30 Jun 2020.
Bhandari, Smitha, MD; Fields, Lisa. "Obsessive-Compulsive Disorder (OCD)." *WebMD*, 4 Sept 2020.
"Bipolar disorder." *Mayo Clinic*, 16 Feb 2021.
Bulthuis, Emily. "Mental illnesses: Terms to use. Terms to avoid." *Health Partners*, 2022.
CBS. "Multiple Personalities." *YouTube*, 8 Mar 2009.
"Classifying eating disorders." *Eating Disorders*.
Faraone, Banaschewski. "What is ADHD?" *Centers for Disease Control and Prevention*, 23 Sept 2021.
Gift From Within- PTSD Resources. "What is a psychopath?" *YouTube*, 9 Nov 2010.
Hoermann, Simone, PH.D. "Wolfgang Amadeus Mozart: Personality Disorder or Bipolar Disorder?" *MentalHelp.net*.

Hwang, Eugene. "What Is Schizophrenia?" *YouTube*, 14 Feb 2016.
Jantz, Gregory L., PhD. "The Anxiety Reset." *Tyndale Momentum*, 2021.
"Mental Disorders." *Medline Plus*, 30 May 2020.
Messer, Lesley. "'Good Will Hunting' turns 20: 9 stories about the making of the film." *ABC News*, 5 December 2017.
"Narcissistic personality disorder." *Mayo Clinic*, 2022.
"Pseudobulbar Affect (PBA)." *Cleveland Clinic*, 2022.
"Serious Mental Illness Prevalence in Jails and Prisons." *Treatment Advocacy Center,* Sept 2016.
Torrey, E. Fuller. "250,000 mentally Ill are Homeless. 140,000 seriously mentally Ill are Homeless." *Mental Illness Policy Org.*
"Victimization and Serious Mental Illness." *Treatment Advocacy Center,* Jun 2016.
Vinney, Cynthia. "What Is Residual Schizophrenia?" *Very Well Mind,* 2 Oct 2021.
Yohanna, Daniel, MD. "Deinstitutionalization of People with Mental Illness: Causes and Consequences." *AMA of Journal Ethics,* Oct 2013.

Memory Loss

King's College London. "New Hope for Hearing Loss Treatment: Researchers Identify 48 Genes Linked to Hearing Loss." *SciTechDaily*, 13 Jun 2022.
Lord Louis Show, The. "18-Minute Analysis By Christopher Nolan On Story & Construction Of Memento." *YouTube*, 19 Sept 2014.
Mayo Clinic Staff. "Dementia." *Mayo Clinic,* 17 Jun 2021.
Mr. nobody. "Memento (2000) | Making of a MASTERPIECE | Christopher Nolan." *YouTube*, 27 Jan 2022.
NPT Reports. "Living with Alzheimer's and Dementia | Aging Matters | NPT." *YouTube*, 1 Jul 2016.

Osmosis. "Alzheimer's disease - plaques, tangles, causes, symptoms & pathology." *YouTube*, 22 Mar 2016.

Motor Impairment

"About." *NeuRA; Motor Impairment Blog.*

Adzick, N. Scott, MD, MMM, FACS, FAAP. "Spina Bifida Causes, Symptoms and Treatment." *Children's Hospital of Philadelphia,* 2022.

Armour, Brian S., PhD; Cahill, Anthony, PhD; Courtney-Long, Elizabeth A., MA, MSPH; Fox, Michael H., ScD; Fredine, Heidi, MPH. "Prevalence and Causes of Paralysis—United States, 2013." *National Library of Medicine,* Oct 2016.

Burr, Pierce; Choudhury, Parichita. "Fine Motor Disability." *National Library of Medicine,* 13 Oct 2021.

"Celebrity Cases of Facial Paralysis." *LA Peer Health Systems*, 2016.

de Groot, Sonja; Ding, Dan; Hansen, Andrew; Jan, Yih-Kuen; Koontz, Alicia M. "Wheeled Mobility." *National Library of Medicine,* 1 Apr 2015.

Di Giovanni, Janine. "The real love story behind The Diving Bell and the Butterfly." *The Guardian,* 29 Nov 2008.

Foster, Cherika; Homol, Lindley. "Lionel Barrymore." *Pennsylvania Center for the Book,* Spring 2007.

Mayo Clinic Staff. "Amyotrophic lateral sclerosis (ALS)." *Mayo Clinic,* 22 Feb 2022.

Mayo Clinic Staff. "Arthritis." *Mayo Clinic,* 15 Sept 2021.

Mayo Clinic Staff. "Essential tremor." *Mayo Clinic,* 4 May 2022.

Mayo Clinic Staff. "Multiple sclerosis." *Mayo Clinic,* 17 Jan 2022.

Mayo Clinic Staff. "Muscular dystrophy." *Mayo Clinic,* 11 Feb 2022.

Normand, Andrew. "Motor Impairments." *The University of Melbourne.*

"What are some types of assistive devices and how are they used?" *National Institute of Child Health and Human Development,* 24 Oct 2018.

"What is Cerebral Palsy?" *Centers for Disease Control and Prevention,* 2 May 2022.

"Why You Don't See More Wheelchair Users in Public." *Spin the Globe,* 2 Aug 2019.

Mutism

Eugene Speech Therapy. "What is a Speech Disorder? (Apraxia of Speech and Dysarthria)." *YouTube,* 23 Jun 2017.

"Learning to Work with Mute Patients in Your Speech-Language Pathology Practice." *Speech Pathology Graduate Programs,* 2022.

Looper. "How Val Kilmer Really Feels About His Top Gun: Maverick Role." *YouTube*, 2 Jun 2022.

"Mutism, Selective." *National Organization for Rare Disorders*, 2011.

Origin. "Raising A Child With Selective Mutism | MY CHILD WON'T TALK | Full Documentary | Origin." *YouTube*, 11 Jan 2019.

Screen Rant Plus. "The Shape of Water Interview: Octavia Spencer and Sally Hawkins." *YouTube,* 7 Dec 2017.

"Surgeons Give Child With No Vocal Cords a Voice." *University of Michigan Health*, 4 Mar 2016.

Deafness

"Aphasia." *National Institute on Deafness and Other Communication Disorders*, 6 Mar 2017.

Cawthon, Stephanie; Garberoglio, Carrie Lou; Palmer, Jeffrey Levi; Sales, Adam. "Deaf People and Employment in the

United States: 2019- General Employment Data." *National Deaf Center*, 2019.

Concha, Pelo. "Family Guy - Dealing With New Female Co Worker and Wife Complaints." *YouTube,* 19 Dec 2015.

"Data and Statistics About Hearing Loss in Children." *Centers for Disease Control and Prevention*, 10 Jun 2021.

Elgaddal, Nazik; Madans, Jennifer H.; Weeks, Julie D. "Hearing Difficulties Among Adults: United States, 2019." *Centers for Disease Control and Prevention*, Jul 2021.

Movies and Television Series

"127 Hours." Boyle, Danny. *Twentieth Century Fox,* 2010.

"Accountant, The." O'Connor, Gavin. *Warner Bros,* 2016.

"Addams Family, The." Sonnenfeld, Barry. *Paramount Pictures,* 1991.

"Alice in Wonderland." Burton, Tim. *Walt Disney Pictures,* 2010.

"Alita: Battle Angel." Rodriguez, Robert. *Twentieth Century Fox,* 2019.

"Amadeus." Forman, Milos. *AMLF,* 1984.

"Amazing Spider-Man, The." Webb, Marc. *Columbia Pictures,* 2012.

"Amazing Spider-Man 2, The." Webb, Marc. *Columbia Pictures,* 2014.

"American Beauty." Mendes, Sam. *DreamWorks Pictures,* 1999.

"AndhaDhun." Raghavan, Sriram. *Viacom18 Motion Pictures,* 2018.

"Army of Darkness." Raimi, Sam. *Renaissance Pictures,* 1992.

"At First Sight." Winkler, Irwin. *MGM,* 1999.

"At the Movies." DuPree, Don. *Buena Vista Television,* 1986-2010.

"Austin Powers in Goldmember." Roach, Jay. *New Line Cinema,* 2002.

"Austin Powers: International Man of Mystery." Roach, Jay. *New Line Cinema,* 1997.

"Austin Powers: The Spy Who Shagged Me." Roach, Jay. *New Line Cinema,* 1999.

"Avatar." Cameron, James. *Twentieth Century Fox,* 2009.

"Avatar: The Last Airbender." DiMartino, Michael Dante; Konietzko, Bryan. *Nickelodeon Animation Studios,* 2005-2008.

"Avengers: Age of Ultron." Whedon, Joss. *Marvel Studios,* 2015.

"Avengers: Infinity War." Russo, Anthony; Russo, Joe. *Marvel Studios,* 2018.

"Aviator, The." Scorsese, Martin. *Warner Bros,* 2004.

"Awakenings." Marshall, Penny. *Columbia Pictures,* 1990.

"Away From Her." Polley, Sarah. *Capri Releasing,* 2006.

"Babel." Iñárritu, Alejandro G. *Paramount Pictures,* 2006.

"Back to the Future." Zemeckis, Robert. *Universal Pictures,* 1985.

"Back to the Future Part II." Zemeckis, Robert. *Universal Pictures,* 1989.

"Back to the Future Part III." Zemeckis, Robert. *Universal Pictures,* 1990.

"Bad Santa." Zwigoff, Terry. *Columbia Pictures,* 2003.

"Ballad of Buster Scruggs, The." Coen, Ethan; Coen, Joel. *Netflix,* 2018.

"Banshees of Inisherin, The." McDonagh, Martin. *Blueprint Pictures,* 2022.

"Barfi!" Basu, Anurag. *UTV Motion Pictures,* 2012.

"Batman and Robin." Schumacher, Joel. *Warner Bros,* 1997.

"Batman." Burton, Tim. *Warner Bros,* 1989.

"Batman Forever." Schumacher, Joel. *Warner Bros,* 1995.

"Batman Returns." Burton, Tim. *Warner Bros,* 1992.

"Batman v. Superman: Dawn of Justice." Snyder, Zack. *Warner Bros,* 2016.

"Beautiful Mind, A." Howard, Ron. *Universal Pictures,* 2001.

"Beauty and the Beast." Condon, Bill. *Walt Disney Pictures,* 2017.

"Beauty and the Beast." Trousdale, Gary; Wise, Kirk. *Walt Disney Pictures,* 1991.

"Best Years of Our Lives, The." Wyler, William. *The Samuel Goldwyn Company,* 1946.

"Big Fish." Burton, Tim. *Columbia Pictures,* 2003.

"Big Lebowski, The." Coen, Ethan; Coen, Joel. *Polygram Filmed Entertainment,* 1998.

"Black Panther." Coogler, Ryan. *Marvel Studios,* 2018.

"Black Swan." Aronofsky, Darren. *Twentieth Century Fox,* 2010.

"Blade Runner." Scott, Ridley. *Warner Bros,* 1982.

"Blade Runner 2049." Villeneuve, Denis. *Sony,* 2017.

"Blindsight." Walker, Lucy. *Robson Entertainment,* 2006.

"Book of Eli, The." Hughes, Albert; Hughes, Allen. *Alcon Entertainment,* 2010.

"Born on the Fourth of July." Stone, Oliver. *Ixtlan,* 1989.

"Boy Who Could Fly, The." Castle, Nick. *Lorimar Motion Pictures,* 1986.

"Bourne Identity, The." Liman, Doug. *Universal Pictures,* 2002.

"Bourne Supremacy, The." Greengrass, Paul. *Universal Pictures,* 2004.

"Bourne Ultimatum, The." Greengrass, Paul. *Universal Pictures,* 2007.

"Brave." Andrews, Mark; Chapman, Brenda; Purcell, Steve. *Pixar Animation Studios,* 2012.

"Braveheart." Gibson, Mel. *Icon Productions,* 1995.

"Breaking the Waves." von Trier, Lars. *Argus Film Produktie,* 1996.

"Bride of Chucky." Yu, Ronny. *Universal Pictures,* 1998.

"Bride of Frankenstein, The." Whale, James. *Universal Pictures,* 1935.

"Bug's Life, A." Lasseter, John; Stanton, Andrew. *Pixar Animation Studios,* 1998.

"Candyman." Rose, Bernard. *PolyGram Filmed Entertainment,* 1992.

"Captain America: The First Avenger." Johnston, Joe. *Marvel Studios,* 2011.

"Captain America: The Winter Soldier." Russo, Anthony; Russo, Joe. *Marvel Studios,* 2014.

"Captain Marvel." Boden, Anna; Fleck, Ryan. *Marvel Studios,* 2019.

"Captain Underpants: The First Epic Movie." Soren, David. *DreamWorks Animation,* 2017.

"Casino Royale." Campbell, Martin. *Columbia Pictures,* 2006.

"Chained for Life." Fraser, Harry L. *Spera Productions Inc,* 1952.

"Charlie and the Chocolate Factory." Burton, Tim. *Warner Bros,* 2005.

"Children of a Lesser God." Haines, Randa. *Paramount Pictures,* 1986.

"Child's Play 2." Lafia, John. *Universal Pictures,* 1990.

"Child's Play 3." Bender, Jack. *Universal Pictures,* 1991.

"Child's Play." Holland, Tom. *United Artists,* 1988.

"Christmas Carol, A." Marin, Edwin L. *MGM,* 1938.

"Christmas Story, A." Clark, Bob. *MGM,* 1983.

"Chronicles of Narnia: Prince Caspian, The." Adamson, Andrew. *Walt Disney Pictures,* 2008.

"Chronicles of Narnia: The Lion, the Witch, and the Wardrobe, The." Adamson, Andrew. *Walt Disney Pictures,* 2005.

"Chronicles of Narnia: The Voyage of the Dawn Treader, The." Apted, Michael. *Walt Disney Pictures,* 2010.

"City Lights." Chaplin, Charles. *Charles Chaplin Productions,* 1931.

"CODA." Heder, Sian. *Apple Original Films,* 2021.

"Coming Home." Ashby, Hal. *Jerome Hellman Productions,* 1978.

"Crip Camp." Lebrecht, James; Newnham, Nicole. *Good Gravy Films,* 2020.

"Cult of Chucky." Mancini, Don. *Universal 1440 Entertainment,* 2017.

"Curious Case of Benjamin Button, The." Fincher, David. *Warner Bros,* 2008.

"Curse of Chucky." Mancini, Don. *Universal 1440 Entertainment,* 2013.

"Cyrano." Wright, Joe. *MGM,* 2022.

"Daredevil." Johnson, Mark Steven. *Twentieth Century Fox,* 2003.

"Dark Knight Rises, The." Nolan, Christopher. *Warner Bros,* 2012.

"Dark Knight, The." Nolan, Christopher. *Warner Bros,* 2008.

"Deadpool 2." Leitch, David. *Twentieth Century Fox,* 2018.

"Deadpool." Miller, Tim. *Twentieth Century Fox,* 2016.

"Deck the Halls." Whitesell, John. *New Regency Productions,* 2006.

"Diamonds Are Forever." Hamilton, Guy. *Eon Productions,* 1971.

"District 9." Blomkamp, Neill. *TriStar Pictures,* 2009.

"Diving Bell and the Butterfly, The." Schnabel, Julian. *Pathé,* 2007.

"Do the Right Thing." Lee, Spike. *40 Acres & A Mule Filmworks,* 1989.

"Don't Breathe." Alvarez, Fede. *Screen Gems,* 2016.

"Donnie Darko." Kelly, Richard. *Pandora Cinema,* 2001.

"Downfall." Hirschbiegel, Oliver. *Constantin Film,* 2004.

"Drake & Josh." Schneider, Dan. *Nickelodeon Productions,* 2004-2007.

"Dr. No." Young, Terence. *Eon Productions,* 1962.

"Dr. Strangelove or: How I Learned to Stop Worrying and Love the Bomb." Kubrick, Stanley. *Stanley Kubrick Productions,* 1964.

"Dracula." Browning, Tod; Freund, Karl. *Universal Pictures,* 1931.

"Drive My Car." Hamaguchi, Ryûsuke. *Bitters End,* 2021.

"Dumbo." Burton, Tim. *Walt Disney Pictures,* 2019.

"Dune." Villeneuve, Denis. *Warner Bros,* 2021.

"E.T. the Extra-Terrestrial." Spielberg, Steven. *Universal Pictures,* 1982.

"Elf." Favreau, Jon. *New Line Cinema,* 2003.

"Elvis." Luhrmann, Baz. *Warner Bros,* 2022.

"Empire Strikes Back, The." Kershner, Irvin. *Lucasfilm,* 1980.

"English Patient, The." Minghella, Anthony. *Miramax,* 1996.

"Eternal Sunshine of the Spotless Mind." Gondry, Michel. *Focus Features,* 2004.

"Eternals." Zhao, Chloé. *Marvel Studios,* 2021.

"Evil Dead II." Raimi, Sam. *Renaissance Pictures,* 1987.

"Evil Dead, The." Raimi, Sam. *Renaissance Pictures,* 1981.

"Extremely Loud and Incredibly Close." Daldry, Stephen. *Warner Bros,* 2011.

"Extreme Makeover: Home Edition." Donahue, Colin; Higgins, Patrick; Taylor, Glenn GT. *ABC,* 2003-2020.

"Fake Beggar, The." Edison, Thomas. *Edison Manufacturing Company,* 1898.
"Family Guy." MacFarlane, Seth; Zuckerman, David. *Fox Television Animation,* 1999-present.
"Family Stone, The." Bezucha, Thomas. *Twentieth Century Fox,* 2005.
"Fantastic Four: Rise of the Silver Surfer." Story, Tim. *Twentieth Century Fox,* 2007.
"Fantastic Four." Story, Tim. *Twentieth Century Fox,* 2005.
"Fatal Attraction." Lyne, Adrian. *Paramount Pictures,* 1987.
"Father Stu." Ross, Rosalind. *CJ Entertainment,* 2022.
"Father, The." Zeller, Florian. *Viewfinder,* 2021.
"Favourite, The." Lanthimos, Yorgos. *Twentieth Century Fox,* 2018.
"Fight Club." Fincher, David. *Twentieth Century Fox,* 1999.
"Finders Keepers." Carberry, Bryan; Tweel, Clay. *Firefly Theater & Films,* 2015.
"Finding Dory." MacLane, Angus; Stanton, Andrew. *Pixar Animation Studios,* 2016.
"Finding Nemo." Stanton, Andrew; Unkrich, Lee. *Pixar Animation Studios,* 2003.
"First Cousin Once Removed." Berliner, Alan. *Experiments in Time, Light & Motion,* 2003.
"Forrest Gump." Zemeckis, Robert. *Paramount Pictures,* 1994.
"For Your Eyes Only." Glen, John. *Eon Productions,* 1981.
"Foster's Home for Imaginary Friends." Affleck, Neil; McCracken, Craig; Shiell, Mike. *Cartoon Network,* 2004-2009.
"Frankenstein." Whale, James. *Universal Pictures,* 1931.
"Freaks." Browning, Tod. *MGM,* 1932.
"Fred Claus." Dobkin, David. *Warner Bros,* 2007.
"Friday." Gray, F. Gary. *New Line Cinema,* 1995.

"Friday the 13th." Cunningham, Sean S. *Paramount Pictures,* 1980.

"From Russia with Love." Young, Terence. *Eon Productions,* 1963.

"Frozen." Buck, Chris; Lee, Jennifer. *Walt Disney Pictures,* 2013.

"Full House." Franklin, Jeff. *Warner Bros. Television,* 1987-1995.

"Fur: An Imaginary Portrait of Diane Arbus." Shainberg, Steven. *River Road Entertainment,* 2006.

"Gattaca." Niccol, Andrew. *Columbia Pictures,* 1997.

"Get Out." Peele, Jordan. *Universal Pictures,* 2017.

"Ghost in the Shell." Oshii, Mamoru. *Manga Entertainment,* 1995.

"Gigot." Kelly, Gene. *Seven Arts Productions,* 1962.

"Girl, Interrupted." Mangold, James. *Columbia Pictures,* 1999.

"Glass." Shyamalan, M. Night. *Universal Pictures,* 2019.

"Godzilla vs. Kong." Wingard, Adam. *Warner Bros,* 2021.

"Goldfinger." Hamilton, Guy. *Eon Productions,* 1964.

"Good Will Hunting." Van Sant, Gus. *Miramax,* 1997.

"Goonies, The." Donner, Richard. *Warner Bros,* 1985.

"Grand Budapest Hotel, The." Anderson, Wes. *Twentieth Century Fox,* 2014.

"Greatest Show on Earth, The." DeMille, Cecil B. *Paramount Pictures,* 1952.

"Greatest Showman, The." Gracey, Michael. *Twentieth Century Fox,* 2017.

"Hannah Montana." Correll, Richard; O'Brien, Barry; Poryes, Michael. *Disney Channel,* 2006-2011.

"Happy Times." Zhang, Yimou. *Guangxi Film Studio,* 2000.

"Harry Potter and the Chamber of Secrets." Columbis, Chris. *Warner Bros,* 2002.

"Harry Potter and the Deathly Hallows: Part 1." Yates, David. *Warner Bros,* 2010.

"Harry Potter and the Deathly Hallows: Part 2." Yates, David. *Warner Bros,* 2011.

"Harry Potter and the Goblet of Fire." Newell, Mike. *Warner Bros,* 2005.

"Harry Potter and the Half-Blood Prince." Yates, David. *Warner Bros,* 2009.

"Harry Potter and the Order of the Phoenix." Yates, David. *Warner Bros,* 2007.

"Harry Potter and the Prisoner of Azkhaban." Cuarón, Alfonso. *Warner Bros,* 2004.

"Harry Potter and the Sorcerer's Stone." Columbis, Chris. *Warner Bros,* 2001.

"Hereditary." Aster, Ari. *Finch Entertainment,* 2018.

"Hobbit: The Battle of the Five Armies, The." Jackson, Peter. *MGM,* 2014.

"Hobbit: The Desolation of Smaug, The." Jackson, Peter. *MGM,* 2013.

"Hobbit: An Unexpected Journey, The." Jackson, Peter. *MGM,* 2012.

"Hook." Spielberg, Steven. *TriStar Pictures,* 1991.

"House of Flying Daggers." Zhang, Yimou. *Beijing New Picture Film,* 2004.

"How the Grinch Stole Christmas." Howard, Ron. *Universal Pictures,* 2000.

"How to Train Your Dragon." DeBlois, Dean; Sanders, Chris. *DreamWorks Animation,* 2010.

"How to Train Your Dragon 2." DeBlois, Dean. *DreamWorks Animation,* 2014.

"How to Train Your Dragon: The Hidden World." DeBlois, Dean; Sanders, Chris. *DreamWorks Animation,* 2019.
"Howard the Duck." Huyck, Willard. *Universal Pictures,* 1986.
"Hunchback of Notre Dame, The." Dieterle, William. *RKO Radio Pictures,* 1939.
"Hush." Flanagan, Mike. *Intrepid Pictures,* 2016.
"I Am Sam." Nelson, Jessie. *New Line Cinema,* 2001.
"iCarly." Schneider, Dan. *Nickelodeon Network,* 2007-2012.
"Ice Age: Collision Course." Chu, Galen T; Thurmeier, Michael. *Twentieth Century Fox,* 2016.
"Ice Age: Continental Drift." Martino, Steve; Thurmeier, Michael. *Twentieth Century Fox,* 2012.
"Ice Age: Dawn of the Dinosaurs." Saldanha, Carlos; Thurmeier, Michael. *Twentieth Century Fox,* 2009.
"Ice Age." Saldanha, Carlos; Wedge, Chris. *Twentieth Century Fox,* 2002.
"Ice Age: The Meltdown." Saldanha, Carlos. *Twentieth Century Fox,* 2006.
"In This Corner of the World." Katabuchi, Sunao. *Mappa,* 2016.
"Incredibles, The." Bird, Brad. *Pixar Animation Studios,* 2004.
"Inspector Gadget." Kellogg, David. *Walt Disney Pictures,* 1999.
"In the Dark." Kingsbury, Corinne. *Warner Bros. Television,* 2019-2022.
"Iron Lady, The." Lloyd, Phyllida. *Pathé,* 2011.
"Iron Man 2." Favreau, Jon. *Marvel Studios,* 2010.
"It's a Wonderful Life." Capra, Frank. *Liberty Films,* 1946.
"Jackass 3D." Tremaine, Jeff. *Dickhouse Productions,* 2010.
"Jackass Forever." Tremaine, Jeff. *Dickhouse Productions,* 2022.
"Jackass Number Two." Tremaine, Jeff. *Dickhouse Productions,* 2006.

"Jackass: The Movie." Tremaine, Jeff. *Dickhouse Productions,* 2002.

"Jackass." Tremaine, Jeff. *Dickhouse Productions,* 2000-2007.

"Jack." Coppola, Francis Ford. *Hollywood Pictures,* 1996.

"Johnny Got His Gun." Trumbo, Dalton. *World Entertainment,* 1971.

"Joker." Phillips, Todd. *Warner Bros,* 2019.

"Kill Bill Vol. 1." Tarantino, Quentin. *Miramax,* 2003.

"Kill Bill Vol. 2." Tarantino, Quentin. *Miramax,* 2004.

"King's Speech, The." Hooper, Tom. *The Weinstein Company,* 2010.

"Kingsman: The Secret Service." Vaughn, Matthew. *Twentieth Century Fox,* 2015.

"Kingsman: The Golden Circle." Vaughn, Matthew. *Twentieth Century Fox,* 2017.

"King's Man, The." Vaughn, Matthew. *Twentieth Century Fox,* 2021.

"L.A. Confidential." Hanson, Curtis. *Warner Bros,* 1997.

"Labyrinth." Henson, Jim. *TriStar Pictures,* 1986.

"Larry King Now." Brown, Scott; Levine, Jonathan M; Smith, M. Ian. *Ora TV,* 2012-2020.

"Lars and the Real Girl." Gillespie, Craig. *MGM,* 2007.

"Leprechaun." Jones, Mark. *Trimark Pictures,* 1993.

"Let Him Go." Bezucha, Thomas. *Mazur/Kaplan Company,* 2020.

"Life Itself." James, Steve. *CNN Films,* 2014.

"Life of Pi." Lee, Ang. *Twentieth Century Fox,* 2012.

"Life on a String." Chen, Kaige. *Beijing Film Studio,* 1991.

"Life, Animated." Williams, Roger Ross. *A&E IndieFilms,* 2016.

"Lighthouse of the Orcas." Olivares, Gerardo. *Wanda Visión S.A,* 2016.

"Lion King, The." Allers, Roger; Minkoff, Rob. *Walt Disney Pictures,* 1994.

"Little Mermaid, The." Clements, Ron; Musker, John. *Walt Disney Pictures,* 1989.

"Little Miss Sunshine." Dayton, Jonathan; Faris, Valerie. *Twentieth Century Fox,* 2006.

"Logan." Mangold, James. *Twentieth Century Fox,* 2017.

"Logan Lucky." Soderbergh, Steven. *Fingerprint Releasing,* 2017.

"Lorax, The." Balda, Kyle; Renaud, Chris. *Universal Pictures,* 2012.

"Lord of the Rings: The Fellowship of the Ring, The." Jackson, Peter. *New Line Cinema,* 2001.

"Lord of the Rings: The Return of the King, The." Jackson, Peter. *New Line Cinema,* 2003.

"Lord of the Rings: The Two Towers, The." Jackson, Peter. *New Line Cinema,* 2002.

"Luca." Casarosa, Enrico. *Pixar Animation Studios,* 2021.

"Mad Max: Fury Road." Miller, George. *Village Roadshow Pictures,* 2015.

"Man Who Laughs, The." Leni, Paul. *Universal Pictures,* 1928.

"Man with the Golden Gun, The." Hamilton, Guy. *Eon Productions,* 1974.

"Many Adventures of Winnie-the-Pooh, The." John Lounsbery; Reitherman, Wolfgang; Sharpsteen, Ben. *Walt Disney Animation Studios,* 1977.

"Mary and Max." Elliot, Adam. *Melodrama Pictures,* 2009.

"Masseurs and a Woman, The." Shimizu, Hiroshi. *Shochiku,* 1938.

"Matilda." DeVito, Danny. *TriStar Pictures,* 1996.

"Matrix Revolutions, The." Wachowski, Lana; Wachowski, Lilly. *Warner Bros,* 2003.

"Matrix, The." Wachowski, Lana; Wachowski, Lilly. *Warner Bros,* 1999.

"Me Before You." Sharrock, Thea. *MGM,* 2016.

"Mean Girls." Waters, Mark. *Paramount Pictures,* 2004.

"Memento." Nolan, Christopher. *Newmarket Capital Group,* 2001.

"Memento." Nolan, Christopher. *Newmarket Capital Group,* 2001.

"Memory of a Killer, The." Van Looy, Erik. *MMG Film & TV Production,* 2003.

"Men in Black." Sonnenfeld, Barry. *Columbia Pictures,* 1997.

"Men, The." Zinnemann, Fred. *Stanley Kramer Productions,* 1950.

"Midnight Cowboy." Schlesinger, John. *Jerome Hellman Productions,* 1969.

"Million Dollar Baby." Eastwood, Clint. *Warner Bros,* 2004.

"Miracle Worker, The." Penn, Arthur. *Playfilm Productions,* 1962.

"Moby Dick." Huston, John. *Moulin Productions Inc,* 1956.

"Monsters vs. Aliens." Letterman, Rob; Vernon, Conrad. *DreamWorks Animation,* 2009.

"Monty Python and the Holy Grail." Gilliam, Terry; Jones, Terry. *Python (Monty) Pictures,* 1975.

"Moon." Jones, Duncan. *Sony Pictures Classics,* 2009.

"Moonstruck." Jewison, Norman. *MGM,* 1987.

"Morbius." Espinosa, Daniel. *Columbia Pictures,* 2022.

"Motherless Brooklyn." Norton, Edward. *Warner Bros,* 2019.

"Mr. Holland's Opus." Herek, Stephen. *Polygram Filmed Entertainment,* 1995.

"Mr. Magoo." Bosustow, Stephen. *UPA,* 1960-1961.

"Mulan." Bancroft, Tony; Cook, Barry. *Walt Disney Pictures,* 1998.

"Muppet Movie, The." Frawley, James. *Henson Associates*, 1979.
"My Left Foot." Sheridan, Jim. *Ferndale Films*, 1989.
"My Name is Khan." Johar, Karan. *Twentieth Century Fox*, 2010.
"My Strange Addiction." Fitzgerald, Joseph R. *20 West Productions*, 2010-2015.
"Never Say Never Again." Kershner, Irvin. *TaliaFilm II Productions*, 1983.
"Nightmare Alley." del Toro, Guillermo. *Fox Searchlight Pictures*, 2021.
"Nightmare on Elm Street, A." Craven, Wes. *New Line Cinema*, 1984.
"No Time to Die." Fukunaga, Cary Joji. *MGM*, 2021.
"Nope." Peele, Jordan. *Universal Pictures*, 2022.
"Nosferatu." Murnau, F.W. *Jofa-Atelier Berlin-Johannisthal*, 1922.
"Notes on Blindness." Middleton, Peter; Spinney, James. *ARTE*, 2016.
"Of Mice and Men." Sinise, Gary. *MGM*, 1992.
"One Flew Over the Cuckoo's Nest." Forman, Milos. *Fantasy Films*, 1975.
"On Golden Pond." Rydell, Mark. *IPC Films*, 1981.
"On Her Majesty's Secret Service." Hunt, Peter R. *Eon Productions*, 1969.
"P.S. I Love You." LaGravenese, Richard. *Alcon Entertainment*, 2007.
"Peanut Butter Falcon, The." Nilson, Tyler; Schwartz, Michael. *Armory Films*, 2019.
"Pearl Harbor." Bay, Michael. *Touchstone Pictures*, 2001.
"Perks of Being a Wallflower, The." Chbosky, Stephen. *Summit Entertainment*, 2012.

"Peter Pan." Geronimi, Clyde; Jackson, Wilfred; Kinney, Jack; Luske, Hamilton. *Walt Disney Animation Studios,* 1953.

"Phantom of the Opera, The." Chaney, Lon; Julian, Rupert; Ernst, Laemmle; Sedgwick, Edward. *Universal Pictures,* 1925.

"Piano, The." Campion, Jane. *CiBy 2000,* 1993.

"Pirates of the Caribbean: At World's End." Verbinski, Gore. *Walt Disney Pictures,* 2007.

"Pirates of the Caribbean: Dead Man's Chest." Verbinski, Gore. *Walt Disney Pictures,* 2006.

"Pirates of the Caribbean: The Curse of the Black Pearl." Verbinski, Gore. *Walt Disney Pictures,* 2003.

"Planet of the Apes." Schaffner, Franklin J. *Twentieth Century Fox,* 1968.

"Pokémon Detective Pikachu." Letterman, Rob. *Warner Bros,* 2019.

"Pokémon Ruby and Sapphire." Masuda, Junichi. *Game Freak,* 2002.

"Poltergeist." Hooper, Tobe. *MGM,* 1982.

"Power Rangers." Israelite, Dean. *Lionsgate,* 2017.

"Prestige, The." Nolan, Christopher. *Warner Bros,* 2006.

"Princess Bride, The." Reiner, Rob. *Act III Communications,* 1987.

"Psycho." Hitchcock, Alfred. *Shamley Productions,* 1960.

"Quiet Place, A." Krasinski, John. *Paramount Pictures,* 2019.

"Quiet Place Part II, A." Krasinski, John. *Paramount Pictures,* 2021.

"Rain Man." Levinson, Barry. *United Artists,* 1988.

"Ratatouille." Bird, Brad; Pinkava, Jan. *Pixar Animation Studios,* 2007.

"Ray." Hackford, Taylor. *Universal Pictures,* 2004.

"Return of the Jedi." Marquand, Richard. *Lucasfilm,* 1983.

"Revenant, The." Iñárritu, Alejandro G. *New Regency Productions,* 2015.

"Robin Hood." Hand, David; Reitherman, Wolfgang. *Walt Disney Animation Studios,* 1973.

"RoboCop." Verhoeven, Paul. *Orion Pictures,* 1987.

"Rogue One: A Star Wars Story." Edwards, Gareth. *Lucasfilm,* 2016.

"Sandlot, The." Evans, David Mickey. *Twentieth Century Fox,* 1993.

"Saving Private Ryan." Spielberg, Steven. *DreamWorks Pictures,* 1998.

"Saw." Wan, James. *Twisted Pictures,* 2004.

"Saw II." Bousman, Darren Lynn. *Twisted Pictures,* 2005.

"Saw III." Bousman, Darren Lynn. *Twisted Pictures,* 2006.

"Saw IV." Bousman, Darren Lynn. *Twisted Pictures,* 2007.

"Saw V." Hackl, David. *Twisted Pictures,* 2008.

"Saw VI." Greutert, Kevin. *Twisted Pictures,* 2009.

"Saw 3D." Greutert, Kevin. *Twisted Pictures,* 2010.

"Scarface." De Palma, Brian. *Universal Pictures,* 1983.

"Scent of a Woman." Brest, Martin. *Universal Pictures,* 1992.

"Schindler's List." Spielberg, Steven. *Universal Pictures,* 1993.

"Seed of Chucky." Mancini, Don. *Rogue Pictures,* 2004.

"See No Evil, Hear No Evil." Hiller, Arthur. *TriStar Pictures,* 1989.

"Separation, A." Farhadi, Asghar. *Memento Films,* 2011.

"Shape of Water, The." del Toro, Guillermo. *Fox Searchlight Pictures,* 2017.

"Shine." Hicks, Scott. *Film Victoria,* 1996.

"Shrek 2." Adamson, Andrew; Asbury, Kelly; Vernon, Conrad. *DreamWorks Animation,* 2004.

"Shrek." Adamson, Andrew; Jenson, Vicky. *DreamWorks Animation,* 2001.

"Shrek Forever After." Mitchell, Mike. *DreamWorks Animation,* 2010.

"Shrek the Third." Hui, Raman; Miller, Chris. *DreamWorks Animation,* 2007.

"Shutter Island." Scorsese, Martin. *Paramount Pictures,* 2010.

"Silence of the Lambs, The." Demme, Jonathan. *Orion Pictures,* 1991.

"Silent Voice, A." Yamada, Naoko. *Shochiku,* 2016.

"Silver Linings Playbook." Russell, David O. *The Weinstein Company,* 2012.

"Simple Simon." Öhman, Andreas. *Naive,* 2010.

"Skyfall." Mendes, Sam. *MGM,* 2012.

"Slumdog Millionaire." Boyle, Danny; Tandan, Loveleen. *MGM,* 2008.

"Snatch." Ritchie, Guy. *Columbia Pictures,* 2000.

"Snow White and the Seven Dwarfs." Cottrell, William; Hand, David; Jackson, Wilfred. *Walt Disney Animation Studios,* 1937.

"Solo: A Star Wars Story." Howard, Ron. *Lucasfilm,* 2018.

"Song of the Sea." Moore, Tomm. *Cartoon Saloon,* 2014.

"Soul Surfer." McNamara, Sean. *Enticing Entertainment,* 2011.

"Sound of Metal." Marder, Darius. *Caviar,* 2020.

"Spaceballs." Brooks, Mel. *MGM,* 1987.

"Spawn." Dippé, Mark A.Z. *New Line Cinema,* 1997.

"Speak." Sharzer, Jessica. *Speak Film Inc,* 2004.

"Spectre." Mendes, Sam. *Columbia Pictures,* 2015.

"Spider-Man 2." Raimi, Sam. *Columbia Pictures,* 2004.

"Spider-Man 3." Raimi, Sam. *Columbia Pictures,* 2007.

"Spider-Man: No Way Home." Watts, Jon. *Marvel Studios,* 2021.

"Spider-Man." Raimi, Sam. *Columbia Pictures,* 2002.

"Spirited Away." Miyazaki, Hayao. Studio Ghibli, 2001

"Splash." Howard, Ron. *Touchstone Pictures,* 1984.
"Split." Shyamalan, M. Night. *Universal Pictures,* 2017.
"SpongeBob SquarePants." Hillenburg, Stephen. *Nickelodeon Animation Studios,* 1999-present.
"Star Wars Episode I: The Phantom Menace." Lucas, George. *Lucasfilm,* 1999.
"Star Wars Episode II: Attack of the Clones." Lucas, George. *Lucasfilm,* 2002.
"Star Wars Episode III: Revenge of the Sith." Lucas, George. *Lucasfilm,* 2005.
"Star Wars." Lucas, George. *Lucasfilm,* 1977.
"Star Wars: The Force Awakens." Abrams, J.J. *Lucasfilm,* 2015.
"Star Wars: The Last Jedi." Johnson, Rian. *Lucasfilm,* 2017.
"Star Wars: The Rise of Skywalker." Abrams, J.J. *Lucasfilm,* 2019.
"Still Alice." Glatzer, Richard; Westmoreland, Wash. *Lutzus-Brown,* 2015.
"Suicide Squad." Ayer, David. *Warner Bros,* 2016.
"Suite Life of Zack and Cody, The." Correll, Richard. *Disney Channel,* 2005-2008.
"Tale of Zatōichi, The." Misumi, Kenji. *Daiei,* 1962.
"Tangled." Greno, Nathan; Howard, Byron. *Walt Disney Pictures,* 2010.
"Tarzan." Buck, Chris; Lima, Kevin. *Walt Disney Pictures,* 1999.
"Teen Titans." Chang, Michael; Jones, Ben; Soto, Alex. *Warner Bros. Animation,* 2003-2006.
"Terminator 2: Judgment Day." Cameron, James. *Carolco Pictures,* 1991.
"Texas Chain Saw Massacre, The." Hooper, Tobe. *Vortex,* 1974.
"Theory of Everything, The." Marsh, James. *Working Title Films,* 2014.
"There's Something About Mary." Farrelly, Bobby; Farrelly, Peter. *Twentieth Century Fox,* 1998.

"There Will Be Blood." Anderson, Paul Thomas. *Paramount Vantage,* 2007.
"Thor: The Dark World." Taylor, Alan. *Marvel Studios,* 2013.
"Thor: Ragnarok." Waititi, Taika. *Marvel Studios,* 2017.
"Three Billboards Outside Ebbing, Missouri." McDonagh, Martin. *Fox Searchlight Pictures,* 2017.
"Three Faces of Eve, The." Johnson, Nunnally. *Twentieth Century Fox,* 1957.
"Thunderball." Young, Terence. *Eon Productions,* 1965.
"Top Gun: Maverick." Kosinski, Joseph. *Paramount Pictures,* 2022.
"Total Recall." Verhoeven, Paul. *Carolco Pictures,* 1990.
"Toy Story 2." Brannon, Ash; Lasseter, John; Unkrich, Lee. *Pixar Animation Studios,* 1999.
"Toy Story." Lasseter, John. *Pixar Animation Studios,* 1995.
"Trading Places." Landis, John. *Paramount Pictures,* 1983.
"Treasure Island." Haskin, Byron. *Walt Disney Productions,* 1950.
"Troll." Buechler, John Carl. *Empire Pictures,* 1986.
"Troll 2." Fragasso, Claudio. *Filmirage,* 1990.
"Unbreakable." Shyamalan, M. Night. *Touchstone Pictures,* 2000.
"Under the Skin." Glazer, Jonathan. *Film4,* 2014.
"Unsane." Soderbergh, Steven. *Fingerprint Releasing,* 2018.
"Upgrade." Whannell, Leigh. *Blumhouse Productions,* 2018.
"Us." Peele, Jordan. *Universal Pictures,* 2019.
"Welcome to Marwen." Zemeckis, Robert. *Universal Pictures,* 2018.
"What About Bob?" Oz, Frank. *Touchstone Pictures,* 1991.
"What Ever Happened to Baby Jane?" Aldrich, Robert. *The Associates & Aldrich Company,* 1962.

"What's Eating Gilbert Grape." Hallström, Lasse. *Paramount Pictures,* 1993.
"Who Framed Roger Rabbit." Zemeckis, Robert. *Touchstone Pictures,* 1988.
"Wild Wild West." Sonnenfeld, Barry. *Warner Bros,* 1999.
"Willow." Howard, Ron. *MGM,* 1988.
"Willy Wonka and the Chocolate Factory." Stuart, Mel. *Wolper Pictures,* 1971.
"Wizard of Oz, The." Cukor, George; Fleming, Victor; LeRoy Mervyn. *MGM,* 1939.
"Wolf Man, The." Waggner, George. *Universal Pictures,* 1941.
"Wolf of Wall Street, The." Scorsese, Martin. *Red Granite Pictures,* 2013.
"Wolverine, The." Mangold, James. *Twentieth Century Fox,* 2013.
"Wonder." Chbosky, Stephen. *Lionsgate,* 2017.
"Wonder Woman." Jenkins, Patty. *Warner Bros,* 2017.
"X2: X-Men United." Singer, Bryan. *Twentieth Century Fox,* 2003.
"X-Men: Apocalypse." Singer, Bryan. *Twentieth Century Fox,* 2016.
"X-Men: Days of Future Past." Singer, Bryan. *Twentieth Century Fox,* 2014.
"X-Men: First Class." Vaughn, Matthew. *Twentieth Century Fox,* 2011.
"X-Men Origins: Wolverine." Hood, Gavin. *Twentieth Century Fox,* 2009.
"X-Men." Singer, Bryan. *Twentieth Century Fox,* 2000.
"X-Men: The Last Stand." Ratner, Brett. *Twentieth Century Fox,* 2006.
"You Only Live Twice." Gilbert, Lewis. *Eon Productions,* 1967.
"Your Name." Shinkai, Makoto. *Toho Company,* 2017.

"Zatōichi." Kitano, Takeshi. *Office Kitano,* 2003.
"Zoey 101." Schneider, Dan. *ApolloProScreen Filmproduktion,* 2005-2008.

Index

"Other" Trope, The, 22, 69, 115
127 Hours, 86, 181
3D Sound Map, 13
Abuse, 97-98, 146
Academy Awards, 48, 67, 73, 97, 153
Accountant, The, 69
Achondroplasia, 30
Acne, 46
Acquired/Delayed Onset, 158
Acuña, Jason "Wee Man", 35
Adaptive Keyboard, 127
Addams Family, The, 35, 86, 179
Affleck, Ben, 69, 96, 97
Agent Smith, 19, 150
Agnelli, Brice, 131
Agoraphobia, 84, 101, 177
Alex Forrest, 99
Alice in Wonderland, 21, 36, 51
Alice Through the Looking Glass, 51
Alita: Battle Angel, 115
Aloysius O'Hare, 36
ALS, 124, 126, 149
Alzheimer's, 108-110, 116-119
Amadeus, 9, 35, 103, 105, 173, 179
Amalric, Mathieu, 128
Amazing Spider-Man 2, The, 51
Amazing Spider-Man, The, 51, 84
American Beauty, 173
American Film Institute, 16
American Sign Language
    ASL, 144, 156-157, 162, 165-166, 168
Americans with Disabilities Act of
    1990, 4, 136, 138
Amnesia, 109, 111
Amniotic Band Syndrome, 78
Amphibian Man, 143-146
Amputation, 78, 79
Amputee, 76-78, 80-81, 84-85, 87-88
AndhaDhun, 24
Anterograde Memory Loss, 112
Antisocial Personality Disorder, 94, 103
Anxiety, 70, 93-94 101, 104, 140, 141-142
Aphasia, 142
Apraxia, 142

Arnie Grape, 67
Arthritis, 126, 136, 177
Arthur, 12
Artificial Limbs. See prosthetic
Ash, 86
Asperger's, 62, 64, 66-67, 69-71
Asylum, 100, 103
Asymmetrical Deafness, 158
At First Sight, 19
Attachment Disorder, 97
Attention-Deficit/Hyperactivity
    Disorder
    ADHD, 94
Audio Description Receiver, 13, 18
Auditory Neuropathy Spectrum
    Disorder, 158
Austin Powers, 35, 36
Autism
    Autistic, 6, 10, 60-74, 93, 140, 145-146, 162, 167, 172, 177, 182
Automatic Page Turner, 127
Avatar, 134, 180
    The Last Airbender, 12, 20, 173
Avengers, 35, 53
Aviator, The, 180
Awakenings, 100, 134, 180
Away From Her, 118
Babel, 161, 163, 180
Back to the Future, 166
Baclanova, Olga, 31
Bacterial Meningitis, 164
Bad Santa, 35
Bale, Christian, 85
Ballad of Buster Scruggs, The, 86, 181
Bane, 45
Banshees of Inisherin, The, 86
Barfi!, 71, 74, 166, 169
Barnell, Jane, 32-33
Barrymore, Lionel, 132
Batman, 36, 44-45, 51, 99
Batman Returns, 36, 51
Batman v. Superman, 84
Bauby, Jean-Dominique, 128-129, 137
Beautiful Mind, A, 101, 180
Beauty and the Beast, 36, 116

Beep Baseball, 13
Belfort, Jordan, 35
Believe It Or Not, 8
Bell's Palsy, 46
Bell's Palsy, 136
Ben Grimm, 22
Ben Sadoun, Florence, 129, 131
Best Picture, 67, 73, 89, 153, 168, 174
Best Years of Our Lives, The, 87, 89
Bible, 21, 64
Big Fish, 37, 179
Big Lebowski, The, 133-134
Big Louie, 84
Bilateral Deafness, 158
Bipolar Disorder, 94
Birth Defects, 78
Black Swan, 101, 181
Blade Runner, 115
Blind, 8, 12-26, 133, 145, 162
Blind Al, 21
Blind Pew, 21
Blindsight, 23, 25
Blofeld, 21, 51
Blood Disease, 179
Book of Eli, The, 20
Bootstrap Bill, 52
Borderline Personality Disorder, 102-103
Born on the Fourth of July, 132, 180
Boy Who Could Fly, The, 69
Braille, 12-14
Brain Disease, 122
Brain injury, 95
Brain Injury, 126
Brave, 86
Braveheart, 9, 35, 54, 57, 85, 180
Breaking the Waves, 135, 137, 180
Bride of Frankenstein, The, 22
Bronchial Pneumonia, 49
Brooks, Mel, 35
Brown, Christy, 132
Browning, Tod, 31-33
Bug's Life, A, 21
Bullet Farmer, 21
Bullet-Tooth Tony, 84
Burden Trope, The, 66

Burton, Tim, 37
Buzz Lightyear, 85
Cancer, 78, 95
Candyman, 84
Cane, 127
Capitol Crawl of 1990, 136
Captain Ahab, 86
Captain America, 51, 117
Captain Davy Jones, 52
Captain Hook, 76, 84, 140
Captain Jack Sparrow, 148
Captain Marvel, 53
Captain Underpants, 36
Cardiac Disease, 126
Cartoon Network, 76
Casino Royale, 21
Catatonia, 94, 100, 134
Caudal Regression Syndrome, 78
Centers for Disease Control and Prevention, 62, 79
Cerebral Palsy, 126
Cerebrovascular Action, 128
CGI, 81
Chained for Life, 179
Chaplin, Charlie, 15-18, 166
Charlie and the Chocolate Factory, 28
Chenoweth, Kristin, 36
Cherrill, Virginia, 15-16
Chief Bromden, 164
Child's Play, 51
Childhood Disintegrative Disorder, 62
Children of a Lesser God, 164, 179
Chirrut Îmwe, 20
Christianity, 82
Christmas Carol, A, 133
Christmas Story, A, 21
Chronicles of Narnia, 35-36, 116
Chuckie, 51
City Lights, 15-16, 18, 25, 131
Clarice Starling, 103
Cleidocranial Dysostosis, 52
Clooney, George, 136
Cochlear Implant, 157, 160-163
Coco, 116
CODA, 161, 165, 168, 181
Colorblind, 151

217

Coma, 129
Coma-Doof Warrior, 21
Comic Con, 50
Comic Relief Trope, The, 21, 35, 53, 69, 86, 117, 133, 148, 166
Coming Home, 133
Conductive Deafness, 158
Congenital Blindness, 14
Congenital Deafness, 158
Congenital High Airway Obstruction Syndrome, 142
Conjoined Twins, 179
Coronavirus
    COVID-19, 163, 168-169, 176
Corpus Colossus, 36
Cousin Itt, 35
Crip Camp, 136, 138
Croze, Marie-Josée, 128
Cruise, Tom, 63, 147
Crutches, 125, 127, 134, 138
Curious Case of Benjamin Button, The, 22, 118, 180
Cyborg, 45, 76
Cyrano, 37, 181
Dafoe, Willem, 85
Damon, Matt, 96-97
Daredevil, 20
Dark Knight, The, 51
Darth Maul, 84
Darth Vader, 51, 84
de la Rouchefoucauld, Sylvie, 129
Deadpool, 21, 52-53, 86
Deaf, 8, 71, 145, 156-170, 176
Death Angel, 160-161, 163, 168
Deck the Halls, 36
Degenerative Brain Disease, 119
del Toro, Guillermo, 143
Dementia, 108, 110, 115, 118, 120, 122, 143
Dependency Trope, The, 165
Dependent Personality Disorder, 103
Depression, 79, 93-94, 103-104, 110, 141
Developmental Disorder, 69, 81, 143
DeVito, Danny, 36-38
Diabetes, 78
Diastrophic, 30
Dinklage, Peter, 35, 37, 42

Diprosopus, 46
Disabled American Veterans Organization, 176
Disease, 8, 17, 36, 48-49, 52, 54, 57, 64-65, 68, 71, 78, 108, 118, 120, 124, 135, 142-143
Disease Trope, The, 52, 68
Disney, 8, 69, 71, 76, 140, 147
Disneyland. See Walt Disney World
Disorganized schizophrenia. See schizophrenia
Disproportionate Dwarfism, 30
Dissociative Identity Disorder, 94, 103, 106
District 9, 52
Diving Bell and the Butterfly, The, 128-129, 131, 137, 147, 180
Do the Right Thing, 178
Doctor Poison, 51
Doll Family, The, 32
Don't Breathe, 21
Donald Pierce, 84
Donnie Darko, 100
Dopey, 148
Dory, 117
Down Syndrome, 6, 9, 64, 110, 176, 178
Downfall, 135, 137
Dr. Claw, 84
Dr. Curtis Connors, 84
Dr. Julius No, 84
Dr. Loveless, 84
Dr. No, 84
Dr. Otto Octavius, 99
Dr. Strangelove, 133
Dracula, 32, 49
Drake & Josh, 182-183
Drive My Car, 152, 154, 181
DUI, 44
Dumbo, 37
Dune, 165
Dwarf
    Dwarfism, 28-30, 38-39
Dysarthria, 142
Dyslexia, 176
E.T., 35, 84
Earles, Daisy, 32
Earles, Harry, 31-32

Eating Disorder, 94
Ebert, Roger, 147
Echolocation, 14
Eckhardt Jr., John, 32
Edison, Thomas, 5
Edna, 36
Elective Mutism. See Selective Mutism
Electroshock Therapy, 177
Elephant Man, The, 36, 47-48, 50, 57, 179
Elf, 28, 39, 41
Elle Driver, 55
Elvis, 37
Emotional Manipulation Trope, The, 67
Emperor Palpatine, 51
English Patient, The, 52, 85, 180
Enrico "Ratso" Rizzo, 135, 137
Essential Tremor, 126
Eternal Sunshine of the Spotless Mind, 118, 121
Eternals, 164
Evil Dead, 86
Ewoks, 35
Extreme Makeover, 9, 77
Extremely Loud and Incredibly Close, 67, 147, 181
Eye Tracking Software, 127
Facebook, 124
Facial Paralysis, 46
Fairbank's Disease, 36
Fake Beggar, The, 5
Familial Alzheimer's. See Alzheimer's
Family Guy, 176
Family Stone, The, 164
Fantastic Four, 22, 45, 52
Fatal Attraction, 99, 179
Father Stu, 132
Father, The, 120, 122, 181
Favourite, The, 136, 138, 181
Fetish Trope, The, 67, 100
Fight Club, 103, 106, 179
Finders Keepers, 88, 90
Finding Dory, 117
Finding Nemo, 117
Fireys, 84
First Cousin Once Removed, 119, 121
Fluctuating Deafness, 158

Fluent Aphasia. See Aphasia
Forbidden Love, 32
Forrest Gump, 80-81, 83, 89, 180
Foster Home, 97
Foster's Home for Imaginary Friends, 76
Frankenstein, 22, 149
Freak, 31, 34, 47, 76, 86, 101, 113
Freak Show, 34, 47, 49
Freaks, 31-34, 41, 53, 85, 131
Fred Claus, 35
Freddy Krueger, 51, 85
Friday, 35
Friedman, Andrea F., 176
Frodo, 85
Frontotemporal Dementia. See Dementia
Frozen, 116
Full House, 109
Fur: An Imaginary Portrait of Diane Arbus, 179
Gattaca, 134
Gazelle, 84
Get Out, 23, 26
Ghost in the Shell, 115
Gibson, Mel, 54
Gigot, 149
Ginarrbrik, 36
Girl, Interrupted, 102, 180
Girma, Haben, 5
Glass, 99, 134
Godzilla vs. Kong, 165, 168
Goldfinger, 149
Gollum, 54, 85, 99
Good Will Hunting, 96, 99, 105, 180
Goonies, The, 52
Gottsagen, Zack, 178
Gout, 136, 138
Grand Budapest Hotel, The, 86
Greatest Show on Earth, The, 36
Greatest Showman, The, 36, 181
Green, Elizabeth, 32
Grumpy Cat, 177
Guide Dog, 14
Guinness World Record, 8, 16
Gynecomastia, 179

219

Hallucination, 115
Hamilton, Bethany, 84
Hanhart Syndrome, 78
Hanks, Tom, 80
Hannah Montana, 183
Hannibal Lecter, 103, 105
Happy Times, 19
Hard of Hearing, 156, 159
Hardwick, Lamar, 7
Harry Osborn, 51, 117
Harry Potter, 9, 28, 35, 51, 84, 86, 116, 134, 173
Harvey Dent, 51
Hawking, Stephen, 124, 132-133, 149, 171
Hawkins, Sally, 143
Head Wand, 127
Hearing Aids, 159, 167
Hearing Loss, 110
Hensel, Abby and Brittany, 176
Hereditary, 52, 115
Hiccup, 84
Hillenburg, Stephen, 124
Hilton, Daisy and Violet, 32
Hitler, Adolf, 135, 137
Hobbit, The, 35
Hoffman, Dustin, 63-64
Hogancamp, Mark, 116
Hoggle, 35
Hook, 116
Hopkins, Anthony, 47, 120
Hopper, 21
Horror Trope, The, 85, 100, 115, 149
Hottle, Kaylee, 165
House of Flying Daggers, 20
How the Grinch Stole Christmas, 28, 35
How to Train Your Dragon, 84
Howard Cliff, 134
Howard the Duck, 35
Hull, John, 26
Hull, John M., 23
Hunchback of Notre Dame, The, 51
Hurt, John, 47-48
Hush, 164
Hypertrichosis, 179
Hypochondria, 101

I Am Sam, 68, 180
iCarly, 183
Ice Age, 178
Ice Bucket Challenge, 124, See ALS
IMDb, 57
Immortan Joe, 55
Imperator Furiosa, 55, 86
In This Corner of the World, 88, 90
Incredibles, The, 36, 84
Industrial Light and Magic, 81
Infection, 78, 95
Inspector Gadget, 84
Inspiration Trope, The, 68, 101, 132, 149
IQ, 68, 80, 89
Iron Lady, The, 181
Iron Man 2, 53
It's a Wonderful Life, 132
Jack, 179
Jackass, 35
James Bond, 21, 149
Jason Bourne, 115
Jason Voorhees, 51
Jawas, 35
Jean-Do. See Bauby, Jean-Dominique
Jenkins, Richard, 143
Jesus, 8, 19, 172
Jim Hudson, 24
Job Accommodation Network, 5
Johnny Got His Gun, 20, 36, 86, 147
Johnson, Tres, 46
Joker, 36, 37, 44, 51, 99, 181
Jolie, Angelina, 136
Joseph, Josephine, 32
Judge Doom, 85
Kanner, Leo, 62
Kanner's Syndrome, 62
Kaysen, Suzanna, 102
Keaton, Buster, 166
Keller, Helen, 22, 165
Kermit the Frog, 178
Kill Bill, 55, 58, 85, 134
Killer Croc, 51
Kilmer, Val, 147
King of Hearts, 36
King's Speech, The, 178, 181
Kingsman, 84

Klaue, 84
Knave of Hearts, 21
Korean Sign Language, 152
Kovic, Ron, 132
Krasinski, John, 160-161, 168
L.A. Confidential, 36
Labyrinth, 35, 84
Lame, 8
Larry King Show, The, 161
Lars and the Real Girl, 100, 180
Larynx, 142, 145
Le Chiffre, 21
Leatherface, 51
Lefou, 36
Legally Blind, 14
Leprechaun, 36
Let Him Go, 86
Leto, Jared, 134
Leukemia, 54, 57
Levels of deafness, 158
Levinson, Barry, 63
Lewy Body, 110
Lieutenant Dan, 80-83, 89
Life Itself, 147
Life of Pi, 173
Life on a String, 23, 25
Life, Animated, 71, 74
Light Perception, 14
Lighthouse of the Orcas, The, 68
Limb Loss, 75, 126, 133
Lion King, The, 21, 69
Lisp, 178
Little Mermaid, The, 147
Little Miss Sunshine, 104, 106, 150, 153
Little People of America, 30, 32
Locked-In Syndrome, 131, 137, See Cerebrovascular Action
Logan, 84, 119
Logan Lucky, 84
Loki, 85
Lollipop Guild, 32
Long John Silver, 84
Long, Stuart, 132
Lorax, The, 36
Lord Farquaad, 38, 41

Lord of the Rings, The, 54, 57, 85, 99, 180
Lord Voldemort, 51
Lou Gehrig's Disease. See ALS
Luca, 86
Lynch, David, 47, 49
Lyutsifer Safin, 51
Macrocephaly, 46, 64
Mad Max, 21, 36, 55, 58, 86
Mad-Eye Moody, 51, 86
Major Depressive Disorder, 104
Makkari, 164
Man Who Laughs, The, 51
Man with the Golden Gun, The, 36
Mangold, James, 120
Manic Depression. See Bipolar Disorder
Marty McFly, 166
Marvel, 35, 51, 53, 84, 86
Marx Brothers, The, 148
Marx, Harpo, 148
Mary and Max, 21, 70, 73, 84, 133
Masseurs and a Woman, The, 19
Matilda, 36
Matlin, Marlee, 161, 176
Matrix Revolutions, The, 19
Matrix, The, 19, 150
McAvoy, James, 99
Me Before You, 133
Mean Girls, 133
Medication, 143
Memento, 111, 112, 121
Memes, 177
Memory Loss, 109, 112-118, 121-122
Memory Loss, 107
Memory of a Killer, The, 118
Men in Black, 9, 115, 117, 173
Men, The, 133
Mental Disorder, 99, 104
Mental Health Disorder, 104
Mental Illnesses, 91, 94
Merrick, John
  Merrick, Joseph, 47-48, 57
Micro Wrestling, 40
32, 45-46, 53
Midget, 29, 34, 40
Midget Boxing, 40
Midnight Cowboy, 135, 137

221

Miles Finch, 39, 41
Million Dollar Baby, 87, 133, 180
Mini-Me, 35-36
Miracle Worker, The, 22, 165
Miramax, 96-97
Mixed Deafness, 158
Moby Dick, 86
Monster Story, The, 32
Monsters vs. Aliens, 179
Monty Python and the Holy Grail, 86
Moon, 115
Moonstruck, 87, 89, 180
Morbius, 134, 179
Morris, Martha, 32
Motherless Brooklyn, 178
Motor Impairment, 125-127, 131-132, 135-138
Mouth Stick, 127
Mr. Freeze, 45
Mr. Glass, 134
Mr. Holland's Opus, 163, 180
Mr. Huph, 36
Mr. Magoo, 144
Mr. Potter, 132, 134
Mr. Strickland, 84, 143-144, 153
Mulan, 36
Multiple Personality Disorder, 94, 104
Multiple Sclerosis, 125-126
Munchkins, 28, 32, 35
Muppet Movie, The, 178
Muscular Atrophy, 32
Muscular Dystrophy, 126
Musculoskeletal Injury, 126
Mute, 8, 140-143, 145, 148-154, 164
My Left Foot, 132, 180
My Name is Khan, 70, 73
My Strange Addiction, 92
Narcissistic Personality Disorder, 94
Nash, Charla, 176
Nash, John, 101
Nature's Mistakes, 32
Neo, 19, 150
Netflix, 12, 164
Neurofibromatosis, 46, 49
Neurogenic Mutism, 142
Nick Fury, 51, 53

Nick Nack, 36
Nickelodeon, 182
Nightmare Alley, 36, 100, 179, 181
Nightmare on Elm Street, A, 51, 85
No Light Perception
   NLP, 14
No Time to Die, 51
Nolan, Christopher, 111-113
Nonfluent Aphasia. See Aphasia
Nope, 53, 176
Norman Bates, 99
Norman Nordstrom, 21
Norman Osborn, 99
Nosferatu, 51
Notes on Blindness, 23, 26
Nurse Ratched, 102, 105
Nyong'o, Lupita, 176
O'Connor, Francis, 32
Obama, Barack, 136
Obama, Michelle, 136
Obesity, 126, 177
Obsessive Compulsive Disorder
   OCD, 94, 101
Obstacle Trope, The, 19, 84, 100, 116, 147, 163
Oddjob, 149
Of Mice and Men, 66
On Golden Pond, 117, 179
One Flew Over the Cuckoo's Nest, 38, 41, 102, 105, 164
Oompa Loompas, 28, 35, 40
Oscar, 19, 89, 124, 168, 174, 179
Oscars, The, 48
Oversized Trackball Mouse, 127
P.S. I Love You, 67
Palsy, 133, 134
Paralysis, 127, 136
Paranoid. See Schizophrenia
Paraplegic, 136
Parkinson's Disease, 110, 126, 135
Patrick Star, 45
PDD-NOS, 60, 62
Peanut Butter Falcon, The, 178
Pearce, Guy, 111
Pearl Harbor, 132
Peek, Kim, 64
Peele, Jordan, 24, 176

Penguin, The, 36, 45, 51
Perks of Being a Wallflower, The, 101
Peter Pan, 36, 76, 84
Peter Pettigrew, 84
Petrificus Totalus, 134
Phantom of the Opera, The, 51
Physical Deformity, 143
Physical Injury, 143
Piano, The, 150, 153, 180
Pinhead, 45
Pirates of the Caribbean, 9, 52, 148
Pity Trope, The, 51, 117, 133
Pixar, 86, 173
Planet of the Apes, 147
Plot Convenience Trope, The, 165
Plot Device Trope, The, 117
Pokémon, 12, 92, 134
Pokémon Detective Pikachu, 115, 134
Poltergeist, 35
Polydactyly, 179
Poor Blood Circulation, 78
Post-lingual Deafness, 158
Power Rangers, 69
Pratt, Chris, 176
Pregnant, 95, 119, 160
Pre-lingual Deafness, 158
Prestige, The, 85, 180
Princess Bride, The, 35, 178-179
Professor Charles Xavier, 119, 134
Professor Poopypants, 36
Professor X. See Professor Charles Xavier
Progeria, 179
Progressive Deafness, 158
Proportionate Dwarfism, 30
Prosthesis. See Prosthetic
Prosthetic, 5, 9, 51, 53, 79, 81-84, 150
Pro-tactile ASL, 157
Proteus Syndrome, 46, 49
Pseudobulbar Affect, 99
Psycho, 99
Psychopath, 94, 95
PTSD, 82, 93, 151, 177
Queen Anne, 136
Quiet Place, A, 160-161, 163, 168-170
Rain Man, 63-66, 73, 180
Randian, Prince, 32

Raoul Silva, 51
Ratatouille, 39, 42
Ray, 19, 180
Red Queen, 51
Red Skull, 51
Redmayne, Eddie, 124
Regina George, 133
Residual Schizophrenia. See Schizophrenia
Respiratory Disease, 126
Retarded, 65, 113
Rett Syndrome, 62
Return of the Jedi, 19
Revenant, The, 86, 181
Ridloff, Lauren, 164
Robert the Bruce, 54
Robin Hood, 19
RoboCop, 9, 115
Roosevelt, Franklin D., 132
Rossitto, Angelo, 32
Sandlot, The, 22
Savant Syndrome, 64
Saving Private Ryan, 87, 90, 132, 180
Saw, 85
Scarface, 21
Scent of a Woman, 20, 180
Schindler, Oskar, 85
Schindler's List, 85, 180
schizophrenia, 94, 95, 100, 101
Schizophrenia, 94
Schlitzie, 32, 54
Schnabel, Julian, 128
Scooter, 127
Screen Reader, 127
See No Evil, Hear No Evil, 166
Seizure, 143
Selective Mutism, 141-142, 148-151
Sensorineural Deafness, 158
Separation, A, 119, 121, 181
Serious Injury, 79
Serma, Oscar, 157
Sexual Harassment, 102
Shape of Water, The, 84, 143, 146, 153, 173, 181
Shapiro, Milly, 52
Shine, 180

223

Shrek, 21, 38, 41, 86
Shutter Island, 100, 134
Siamese Twins, 34
Sign Language, 150, 154, 160, 162
Silence of the Lambs, The, 103, 105
Silent Voice, A, 167, 170
Silver Linings Playbook, 101, 181
Simmonds, Millicent, 160, 162, 176
Simple Simon, 71, 73
Single-Switch Access, 127
Sinise, Gary, 81, 176
Sip and Puff Switch, 127
Siskel and Ebert, 64
Skinner, 39, 42
Skyfall, 51
Sloth, 52
Slumdog Millionaire, 20
Smeagol, 54, 57
Smee, 36
Snatch, 84
Snellen Chart, 14
Snow White and the Seven Dwarfs, 148
Snow, Elvira, 32
Snow, Jenny Lee, 32
Social Anxiety, 147
Sociopath, 95
Solo: A Star Wars Story, 84
Song of the Sea, 151, 153
Soul Surfer, 84
Sound of Metal, 167, 170, 181
Spaceballs, 35
Spasmodic Dysphonia, 179
Spawn, 52
Speak, 147
Spectre, 51
Speech Delay, 60, 61, 71, 140
Spider-Man, 99, 116
Spider-Man 2, 99
Spider-Man 3, 117
Spielberg, Steven, 87
Spina Bifida, 126
Spinal Cord injury, 127
Spirited Away, 116
Splash, 148
Split, 99

Spondyloepiphyseal Dysplasias, 30
SpongeBob SquarePants, 45, 92, 124
Sporadic Alzheimer's. See Alzheimer's
Sprague, Isaac W., 32
Stable Deafness, 158
Stallone, Sylvester, 136
Stammering, 141
Star Wars, 9, 20, 35, 51, 84, 115, 178
Stewart, Kristen, 147
Still Alice, 116, 181
Stroke, 126, 127, 143
Stutter, 178
Sudden Deafness, 158
Suicide, 6, 15, 93, 97, 99, 101, 104, 114, 133, 135, 167, 170
Suicide Squad, 51
Suite Life of Zack and Cody, The, 183
Sullivan, Anne, 22, 165
Superhuman Trope, The, 20, 52, 69, 134, 164
Superman, 52
Supreme Leader Snoke, 51
Surgery, 125, 143, 147, 158
Suskind, Owen, 71
Sweet Anita, 177
Sybil, 104
Symmetrical Deafness, 158
Tadoma Speechreading Method, 157
Tale of Zatoichi, The, 19
Tangled, 36
TAR Syndrome, 78
Tarzan, 36
Teen Titans, 45, 76
Terminator 2: Judgment Day, 173
Tethered, 56, 151, 154
Texas Chainsaw Massacre, The, 51
Text-to-Speech, 13
Theory of Everything, The, 124, 132, 149, 181
Therapy, 60, 97-98, 105, 140
There Will Be Blood, 166, 169, 180
There's Something About Mary, 69
Thing, The, 22, 45
Thor, 51, 53, 85
Three Billboards Outside Ebbing, Missouri, 39, 42, 181
Three Faces of Eve, The, 100

Throat Cancer, 147
Thyroid Cancer, 147
TikTok, 177
Tiny Tim, 133
Tissue Damage, 79
TLC, 92
Tony Montana, 21
Toothless, 84
Top Gun: Maverick, 147
Toph, 12, 20
Total Mutism. See Selective Mutism
Total Recall, 115
Toughness Trope, The, 51, 86
Tourette's, 177, 178
Toy Story, 85
Toy Story 2, 85
Trading Places, 21, 133
Trauma, 51, 90, 93, 98, 148, 169, 172
Traumatic Brain Injury, 110
Traumatic injury, 46
Treacher Collins Syndrome, 46, 52
Treasure Island, 21, 84
Treves, Frederick, 47
Troll, 35
Troll 2, 35
Tunnel Vision, 14
Turner Syndrome, 30
Twitch, 177
Two-Face, 45
Ugly Laws, 176
UHF, 84
Unbreakable, 134
Under the Skin, 53
Underminer, The, 84
Undifferentiated Schizophrenia. See Schizophrenia
Unilateral Deafness, 158
Unsane, 102
Upgrade, 134
Us, 56, 58, 151, 154, 173, 179
Vaccine, 68, 177
Van Sant, Gus, 96
Vascular, 78, 110
Vascular Disease, 78
Victim Trope, The, 19, 37, 53, 85, 118, 147, 164

Villain Trope, The, 21, 36, 51, 84, 99, 134
Virchow-Seckel Syndrome, 32
Voice Recognition Software, 127
Walker, 127
Wallace Keefe, 84
Wallace, William, 54
Walt Disney World, 8, 140
Welcome to Marwen, 116
What About Bob?, 101
What Ever Happened to Baby Jane?, 133
What's Eating Gilbert Grape, 67, 180
Wheaton Center for Faith and Disability, 176
Wheelchair, 5, 77, 80, 82, 125, 127, 130, 133, 134, 136, 138, 176
Whisnant, Shannon, 88
White Cane, 14
Who Framed Roger Rabbit, 85
Wicked Witch of the West, The, 106
Wild Wild West, 84
Wilder, Gene, 132
Will Turner, 52
Williams, Robin, 96, 98-99, 124
Willow, 35
Willy Wonka and the Chocolate Factory, 35, 132, 166
Winnie-the-Pooh, 104
Winter Soldier, The, 86, 117
Wizard of Oz, The, 28, 32, 35, 106
Wolf Man, 49
Wolf of Wall Street, The, 35, 181
Wolverine. See Logan
Wonder, 51, 181
Wonder Woman, 51
Wood, John, 88
Woody, 85
Woolsey, Minnie, 32
Wright, Robin, 80
X-Men, 119, 122, 134
Yao, 36
Your Name., 116
YouTube, 92, 172
Zatōichi, 19, 211
Zemeckis, Robert, 80
Zoey 101, 183

Made in the USA
Coppell, TX
09 December 2022